Living with Emetophobia

of related interest

Cutting it Out
A Journey through Psychotherapy and Self-Harm
Carolyn Smith
Foreword by Maggie Turp
ISBN 978 1 84310 266 3

Washing My Life Away
Surviving Obsessive-Compulsive Disorder
Ruth Deane
ISBN 978 1 84310 333 2

In and Out of Anorexia
The Story of the Client, the Therapist and the Process of Recovery
Tammie Ronen and Ayelet
ISBN 978 1 85302 990 5

A Systemic Treatment of Bulimia Nervosa
Women in Transition
Carole Kayrooz
Foreword by a Service User
ISBN 978 1 85302 918 9

Living with Emetophobia

Coping with Extreme Fear of Vomiting

Nicolette Heaton-Harris

Foreword by Linda Dean

Jessica Kingsley Publishers
London and Philadelphia

First published in 2007
by Jessica Kingsley Publishers
116 Pentonville Road
London N1 9JB, UK
and
400 Market Street, Suite 400
Philadelphia, PA 19106, USA

www.jkp.com

Printed digitally since 2009

Disclaimer

The advice in this book does not constitute medical advice and does not attempt to replace therapy or treatment by a professional. Always seek professional advice from a qualified therapist or medical practitioner.

Library of Congress Cataloging in Publication Data

Heaton-Harris, Nicolette.

Living with emetophobia : coping with extreme fear of vomiting / Nicolette Heaton-Harris ; foreword by Linda Dean.

p. cm.

ISBN 978-1-84310-536-7 (pb : alk. paper) 1. Emetophobia--Popular works. I. Title.

RC552.E44H43 2007

616.85'225--dc22

2007012307

British Library Cataloguing in Publication Data

A CIP catalogue record for this book is available from the British Library

ISBN 978 1 84310 536 7

To all emetophobics and those that support them. For Jackie, my newfound friend. For my parents, who did their best. Last, but not least, to my husband Nicholas who listened to me when I first told him and never judged, for supporting me and being the one to do the clearing up when the kids get ill. Thank you.

Contents

Foreword

'But nobody likes being sick!' This is the usual response from anyone who hears the words 'vomit phobia' yet these people are not aware of how far-reaching the effects of the phobia can be or how they can take over a person's life. Back in 1992–3 when Gut Reaction was formed, the term 'emetophobia' (a fear of oneself or others vomiting) was barely heard of. I recall approaching the medical profession where it was met by blank expressions as they quizzically asked what emetophobia is. How the profile of emetophobia has changed since the Dark Ages of 1993. Today it is often included in listings of the most common phobias, usually at around the fifth or sixth position following the most widely acknowledged phobias such as agoraphobia, social phobia and arachnaphobia (spiders).

Emetophobics mostly fall into two groups – those who predominantly fear themselves vomiting and those who mostly fear others vomiting – but there is usually some overlap between the two. Either way, it can be a most disabling condition affecting almost every aspect of a sufferer's life, even including eating, as many emetophobes who fear themselves vomiting eat a very restricted 'safe' diet. Some women will avoid pregnancy with its risks of morning sickness and those who do go ahead often dread having to care for an unwell child. Many live their daily lives in dread, monitoring every internal twinge for any signs of nausea and should there be any stomach bugs circulating then they can become a virtual recluse in their homes. Unfortunately, because the fear is of an internal illness or symptom, unlike other phobias it is not possible to avoid it completely. Consequently, many emetophobes with a fear of themselves vomiting can suffer from the fear almost constantly and those who fear others vomiting may restrict their social lives to minimise their risks of seeing anyone vomiting.

Unlike other phobias it is not usually possible to confront it on a gradual basis via systematic desensitisation, the method often used to treat other phobias. In many cases, confronting the phobia via vomiting can actually serve to reinforce it. Thus it can be a complex condition to treat effectively and the phobia can persist for years, having a tremendous negative impact upon its sufferers' lives.

It is seldom a pleasant subject to discuss or read about, yet it is only by raising the profile of the phobia that it becomes a recognised condition gaining acceptance and acknowledgement within the medical profession and, it is hoped, leading to research into effective treatments and a possible cure in the future.

Linda Dean
Founder of Gut Reaction

Introduction

For me, the decision to write this book was clear. I was so fed up with other people not knowing what emetophobia was. They never understood what it meant. I'd say, 'I have emetophobia' and they'd say, 'What's that?' After a quick explanation that always seemed to make me feel a little embarrassed, they misinterpreted what I meant and assumed it was something that would pass, that it was something trivial or, even worse, say, 'Oh, I used to be like that,' when quite clearly, if they had used to be like that, then they wouldn't have needed the explanation in the first place. It seemed that anyone who heard about a vomit phobic would then say that they used to hate being sick and would then assume that they were emetophobic. Well, it doesn't work like that.

I also felt that it was imperative for more people to know about emetophobia. Not just doctors, counsellors and therapists, but friends, family and colleagues. There was an inherent need for the information about emetophobia to be brought clearly into the open. It is such a secretive phobia; not secretive in the way anorexia or bulimia are secretive, but secretive because sufferers want people to know how they feel and why, but they are generally too terrified or scared to tell them. The embarrassment of telling someone, yet again, that you're emetophobic only sets off a long chain of questions from the people you've just told. They don't know what emetophobia is. They think it only affects you when you feel ill. They don't realise the impact it has on your life and the strategies you have to come up with just to pretend that everything is normal, which it is.

Emetophobes are scared of getting sick, of vomiting. This fear envelops every aspect of their lives to such a degree that some phobics are suicidal. Yes, they'd rather take their own life than vomit. Extreme? Maybe, but emetophobes' worrying thoughts can invade their minds constantly, leaving them on a persistent edge of worry, stress and anxiety. Imagine living that way, 24 hours a day, with little sleep and the parameters of your life being controlled by a phobia.

This book needed to be written. It also needs to be read by everyone and anyone – emetophobes, doctors, social workers, teachers – because then, when someone tells you he or she is emetophobic, you'll be able to nod your head and understand just how that person is feeling without him or her having to go through it all over again. Sufferers won't suffer with having to feel embarrassed that you won't know what they're going on about. They'll get help, and we all need a little of that.

In this book, you'll read about some of the extremes that some emetophobes go to. Like any phobia, it has a vast spectrum of suffering. Some emetophobes are able to hold down jobs, live their lives and generally cope and they are normal, happy people. But there are other emets who have all the extremes. They are suicidal or keep their phobia to themselves. There are also emets somewhere in between these two states. As I said, there's a spectrum, but having said that, we need to know and realise just how all-encompassing this phobia is or can be to a phobic. This book will do exactly that.

Nicolette Heaton-Harris
January 2007

A note on the text

All names of individuals mentioned in this book have been changed.

CHAPTER ONE

What is Emetophobia?

When the little blue line appeared, I couldn't believe it. I was pregnant! For a very brief moment, I was thrilled to bits. This was my wildest dream come true. But then, reality set in and then the fear. If I was pregnant, then that meant I'd probably suffer with morning sickness and I knew from research and talking to others that it could last for the first three months or even throughout the whole nine!

I couldn't do it. I just knew I didn't have the courage, or the strength. Already, just thinking about it, I was beginning to feel sick, so I knew I had to act fast.

I made an appointment for an abortion. If I got it out of me quick enough then the morning sickness wouldn't get me. I didn't tell Richard. How could I? He knew nothing of my phobia and I knew how much he wanted kids.

So I went to the clinic on my own. I was terrified and asked to be awake whilst they scraped the baby out of me. I didn't want to risk a general anaesthetic because of the after-effects. So I lay there, listening to the noises in the operating theatre and staring at the ceiling, praying for it all to be over. When I got taken back to my room, the sense of relief that I wouldn't get sick was immense, but it competed with the strong grief that was tearing through me. I'd killed a baby because of my fear. How awful was I?

> Soon after, I began cutting myself to release the pain inside. Seeing the trickles of blood running down my arm helped a lot and once I even put a knife to my heart to end it all, I hurt so much inside with the knowledge of what I'd done. But I couldn't do it. You know why? Because if I didn't do it properly, stab myself, and Richard found me, I knew I'd get taken to hospital. That I'd be operated on. Be given a general anaesthetic and get sick that way. I feel pathetic. I can't even kill myself. It's too risky. I fear being sick more than dying. How screwed up is that?
>
> I light a little candle on what would have been that baby's birthday every year and I cry to myself. Richard suspects I'm upset, but he doesn't pry. He figures I'll tell him in my own sweet time. But I don't think he'll understand. He's asking about us starting to have kids. How do I tell him I've already got rid of one? Because I don't think he'll understand. How could he when I don't? (Emma, 28)

So what *exactly* is emetophobia? Apart from it being an extreme fear of sickness and vomiting, it is also powerful. This phobia is so life-encompassing. It affects sufferers in everything they do, all day long. Someone who is a non-emet may say, 'Well no one likes being sick.' Yes, that is true, but to an emetophobe it is much more than that. The phobia doesn't just affect sufferers when they feel unwell or see someone else is unwell, it affects them every hour of every day. There is the constant worry, the anxiety, the stress about catching a bug, of seeing someone be sick in public, of hearing a colleague mention that his or her child was poorly during the night or of hearing that there's a bug going round. One of the biggest concerns and worst times of the year for an emetophobe is the season for the winter vomiting bug (Norovirus), when a lot of emetophobes refuse to leave their homes or allow anyone to enter them from about November through to May, when they might deem it 'safe'.

An emetophobe is usually extremely underweight. Many of them are on anti-anxiety medications. Some self-harm or are suicidal. Emetophobia is one of the top five phobias, yet little is known about it because sufferers are so secretive. They assume they are alone in the world and many of them don't realise that there are others like them until they reach their thirties or even their forties.

> I used to lie awake every night, shivering and shaking, panic tearing me apart because I felt so ill and I'd wake in the mornings after having fallen asleep eventually through nervous exhaustion. I'd never heard of anyone else like me. I thought there was something wrong with me but the doctors just said I was just a naturally anxious person. I said it was more than that, that it was this sickness thing, but he had no idea what I was talking about. It made me think that if the doctors didn't know about it, then I had to be the only one... I'm on Prozac now. My life's a mess. (Tina, 46)

Sadly, Tina's situation is not unique. Many medical professionals, including counsellors and therapists, have never heard of emetophobia and those that have do not yet have the 'cure' that all emetophobes seek. All emetophobes want is to live a normal life like everyone else. They don't want the fear, they don't enjoy it. It's not like arachnophobia (a fear of spiders) where sufferers can escape if they see a spider in the room. The thing causing emetophobes' fear is inside of them; their stomach. You can't run away from that – it's part of you. This is why many emetophobes cut themselves and self-harm. It's a way of punishing the body for what it is doing to them. It releases the tension building up to catastrophic levels inside.

Because of this phobia, many emetophobes feel so much pressure and fear on a daily basis that they are unable to hold down a full-time job. Being surrounded by so many people, some who might have been ill or have children who could have caught a bug from school, is just too much. They eavesdrop on conversations, not because they're nosy and want to gossip but because they're trying to protect themselves. They need to know that the people sitting near them or standing next to them haven't been ill. If they have, then they'll start to panic that they'll get sick next and need to get away. Many emetophobes have lost their jobs because of the amount of sick leave they've taken, so many just have part-time positions or no job at all because it's safer.

Relationships can also be affected:

> I met this wonderful girl who lit up my life. I'd been suffering with the emet for years and was beginning to think I'd be single all my life when she dazzled me with her smile and good nature...but it was too good to be true. There was a reason she was such the life and soul. Tammy was a drunk. And even though she was a happy drunk and great to be with she would often be sick and I couldn't stand laying in bed listening to her heave and vomit in the bathroom all night long. On our third night together, she spent most of it in the bathroom being sick and when she came out she looked like death warmed up. I knew she didn't have a bug and that the sickness was caused by booze, but I couldn't stand to be around her any more. I left her. She was stunned and doesn't know the real reason why. (Keith, 36)

Stories like Keith's abound in the emet community. Many female emets who 'faced the gauntlet of morning sickness' and are mothers, actually move out of their homes when their children catch a bug at school. They feel for their children and ache to comfort them like any parent would, but are terrified of being near them. One mother wrote to say that she camped out in the back garden leaving her husband to take care of their son who was being violently ill while she 'shivered with fear' and berated herself for being so selfish and cowardly.

Emetophobia is like this. It is an incredibly strong phobia. It has a powerful hold and once it's there you have to find ways of coping with it. But how? And how do you deal with the reactions of people who think you're just over-reacting? Read on and this book will tell you how and it will also show you how to cope with those times when the emetophobia envelops you.

> I'm sick of this fear. I'm sick of the sickness. I want it all to be over. If my doctor doesn't help me soon, then I just know I'm going to do something drastic. Someone help me...please! (Sherry, 13)

Types of emetophobia

The UK's premier site for emetophobes, providing information and support, is called Gut Reaction (see Organisations and online resources, p.157), founded by emet sufferer Linda Dean. On the site, she explains the two main types of emetophobic sufferers in simple terms:

> Emetophobes fall into two categories:
>
> - Those who primarily fear *themselves* vomiting and
> - Those who primarily fear *others* vomiting.[1]

Of course, like any illness, mental or otherwise, there are many varying levels among each type. I would argue that there is a third type – those who fear both *themselves and others* vomiting. Each of these types is then divided into 'anxiety-based' sufferers and 'nausea-based' sufferers.

Anxiety-based sufferers already have an underlying anxiety, usually accompanied by strong panic attacks, mild agoraphobia and social phobia. Their anxiety leads to nausea, which (in a vicious circle) causes stronger panic attacks, increased feelings of sickness and physical shaking.

---

1 Dean, L. (2007) *What is Emetophobia?* Gut Reaction. Available at www.gutreaction.freeserve.co.uk/emetophobia.htm. Reprinted with permission.

Nausea-based sufferers are those with a physical illness that causes symptoms of nausea. This nausea then triggers their phobic reaction to the sensations of sickness, which in turn leads to more anxiety and further symptoms of nausea (Gut Reaction 1999–2006).

Recognising emetophobia

So how would an ordinary person, or doctor, or counsellor, spot an emetophobic sufferer? It's difficult. Unless the person with emet chooses to tell you, it would be highly unlikely that anyone would spot one, at least in today's climate. Even though emetophobia is one of the most common phobias, it is hardly known about. Emets guard their phobia for many reasons. Perhaps 'guard' is the wrong word. Most emets tend to think that they are the only one like it and many have reported that they only learnt there were others like them when they were in their thirties or later. (With the widespread use of the Internet, younger emets are now discovering there are thousands like them all across the globe.)

Sufferers are highly skilled at making excuses when they are put in situations that they feel will threaten them with their worst nightmare – sickness and vomiting. If tasks or events are suggested which emets feel will put them at risk or expose them to infection, they are quick to think up some excuse that will get them out of the situation. It's almost an instinct of self-preservation. If this seems an exaggeration, be aware that most emets feel that being sick – actually throwing up – is worse than dying.

Indicators for family members to look out and for doctors to be aware of are habitual patterns of avoidance. This avoidance can be around what many people may consider run-of-the-mill life situations such as avoiding public transport or insisting on being the driver of their own car whilst others in a group travel by train or bus. They will often refuse to travel by boat or aeroplane, never going abroad or on holiday to strange destinations.

Fairgrounds and theme parks are definite no-go areas due to the risk of seeing others being ill after a particularly dizzying ride.

Sufferers also adopt highly meticulous food hygiene. They have rules about what they will eat and what they deem 'safe'. They have even been known to inspect a restaurant kitchen before ordering a dish (that is if you have managed to get them out in the first place). The majority of emets will eat foods that they don't have to touch with their fingers, but largely consider 'finger foods' as the safest. This usually means that they eat food straight from its wrapping without touching it or, if they have to touch it, will eat most of a sandwich but throw away the corner that they have been holding. Many emets have a diet they consider 'safe' such as well-washed fruit and vegetables that couldn't possibly give them food poisoning. Crisps, biscuits and sandwiches are usually also considered safe. Cooked food will be dissected carefully to check that it has cooked all the way through. The slightest hint of pink in chicken will mean that it won't be touched, nor any of the food touching the chicken, in case of contamination.

Medical treatment

Medical treatment is often avoided, even if it could mean saving their lives. The idea of going into a doctor's surgery for an appointment is anathema. If they are forced to go, they will choose to sit by an open window to breathe 'clean' air. They won't touch anything, won't read a magazine in case it has been touched by someone ill, won't lick their lips in case germs adhere to their mouths and they often try to breathe shallowly through the nose:

> Whenever I had to go to the doctor as a child, I'd refuse to sit in the waiting room and I'd wait in my mum's car. She had to sit inside and come fetch me when they called my name. I'd take a deep breath outside and then rush through to the doctor's room, trying not to touch the door

> handles or anything. The doctor said my blood pressure was always high when I was there and he could hardly hear what I was saying because I was hardly daring to breathe in. I couldn't wait to get out of there and when I did, I'd still spend the next week or so waiting to come down with any bug I may have picked up. (Rachel, 19)

Medical procedures such as surgery that involve general anaesthesia are considered such an awful prospect that most emets will try all other routes before considering it, often turning down the surgery anyway, despite the repercussions.

Prescribed medicines will only be taken after an emetophobe has rigorously checked the information leaflet that comes with them for their side effects. If the side effects list nausea, sickness or vomiting, then the medication will not be taken.

Many female emets will not consider pregnancy because of the morning sickness and some will starve themselves when others in their homes are ill. These emets are often misdiagnosed as suffering with anorexia nervosa. Emets can be socially isolated and afraid of leaving their homes. If they do, they may spend their time watching out for others who may be ill or listening out for anyone coughing or choking. These socially isolated emets also seem to develop agoraphobia (a fear of going outside) or social phobia (a fear of being around other people). Despite their fear of vomiting, it seems that most emets have a high 'vomit continence' and can fight the requirement to vomit until the nausea passes.

An emet sufferer is not only in danger of developing other phobias, but is also at high risk of developing an obsessive compulsive disorder, the most obvious one being excessive hand-washing.

Of course not all emets will have all of these avoidance behaviours. Some have one or two, some have all of them and more. To a 'normal' person, these behaviours may seem ridiculous or even something to laugh about. For this reason most emetophobes keep quiet about their fears, but to a sufferer the terror is extremely real. Being sick is the worst possible thing they can imagine happening to them. They know it is irrational; they know it is not logical. Emetophobes are not stupid, or uneducated; in fact, many are intelligent and empathic. Yet they cannot get past this fear. It is insurmountable. It seems too much to deal with on a daily basis. Everything in their lives can seem connected to their fear in some small way and each extra piece of anxiety builds and builds up inside them until some emets harm themselves or consider suicide as the only way out. Thankfully, these are few. Most emets get themselves to a doctor and obtain medication for depression or anxiety (which they'll take only if the side effects don't include nausea/vomiting).

Emetophobia is with the sufferers every second of the day, every breath they take, and the relentless fear and anxiety pulls them down. The information provided by this book should educate everyone who reads it. To those without emetophobia, please have some understanding. Don't dismiss the fear as 'nothing'; it needs to be taken seriously. To those with emetophobia, know that you are not alone. There are coping strategies you can employ to get you through each day. There are people who can help, who will support you, but you have to speak out and tell people – the way this book is doing – or no one is going to know how you really feel.

CHAPTER TWO

My Story

So you may be asking yourself what qualifications I have to write this book. How do I think I know everything there is to know about emetophobia? Well, I'm sure I don't know everything. Each day I am surprised by something new I learn from other emetophobes. But my qualifications? I've been emetophobic since I was a child and three decades later I'm still suffering with it along with my eldest son.

Where it all started

I was the youngest of four children and my first memory of being sick is when I was about seven or eight years old. I had a stomach ache that day, yet despite this my mum, who was learning to swim, took us all to the swimming pool to splash about while she had her lesson. I sat on the side with my dad, who worked there as a pool supervisor and lifeguard. I was feeling pretty ill, but I can't remember feeling scared. The ache got worse and I told my dad, who said, 'Tell your mum.' So I got off his knee and went over to the splash pool to get her attention. 'Mum, my tummy hurts.'

My mum sighed and told me to go and wait with my dad. She would be finishing soon enough. I went back to sit with my father and the second I sat on his knee I threw up. I can remember feeling as if my eyes would burst out of my head at this strange, awful, violent reaction that I'd never experienced before. The taste was awful and I was vaguely aware of swimmers in the nearby pool screaming in horror as my vomit splashed onto the poolside. In those days a siren would sound to alert swimmers that their time in the pool had ended. As my dad led me through to the nearest sink next to the basket room, I heard the siren going off and all the other lifeguards shouting at people to evacuate the pool.

I was leaning over the sink, trying to breathe, but nothing was happening. My stomach was cramping in painful waves and my eyes were burning with tears. My dad stood beside me encouraging me to cough it all up. I tried to tell him I couldn't but I didn't have a voice. I couldn't breathe. I couldn't speak. I seemed stuck in a terrifying limbo. My legs began to shake and I thought that this was how people felt before they died.

Then suddenly it stopped. Air rushed into my lungs, the stomach cramps disappeared and I could breathe again. I began to cry and my dad helped me wash my mouth and showed me how to rinse it out. I practically limped out of the leisure centre, seeing all these people, wrapped in their towels, staring at me as I passed. Dad put me in the car outside and told me to wait for Mum and my brothers. One of Dad's colleagues, a lovely lady called Dot, came to the car and gave me five pence to spend on sweeties when I was feeling better. I clutched it tightly and laid my head against the window, feeling a little dizzy. Later I learned that they had turfed everyone out of the pool so they could clean it down. About fifty swimmers had been displaced by me.

It was after this event that the fear took hold. I learned that what had happened to me was called 'being sick'. I can type the word and read it now without it bothering me – sick – but back then, learning about it, experiencing it, I seemed to see it everywhere. Every book I read (and I was a voracious reader) seemed to have the word in it, or a word like it: pick, lick, chick, thick. If I saw words that ended in -ick my mind automatically superimposed the letter s at the front and the whole event replayed itself vividly in my mind and churned my stomach. I stopped reading.

I noticed that the word and others like it were also on television. If I heard them I'd feel like curling up tight, like a foetus, and hiding. I honestly thought that it would happen to me again if I heard the word or read it. I thought I was going mad. But who could I tell? They would think I was silly and being a little girl. I had three older brothers, boisterous boys to whom a little illness was nothing. So I hid the fear, like a shameful secret, but even though it was locked away and I tried not to pay it any attention, it seemed to grow.

Because I'd been sick away from home, my house became my safe haven. It seemed easier there and I panicked every time I had to go out. No one knew. I hid it well. But sometimes it would overwhelm me and my dad would be furious that everywhere we went 'our Nikki's always rushing us about'. He had this idea once to take us all out for a meal at a restaurant. I was excited, yet nervous. I wanted to experience going out for a meal, yet I didn't want to leave home. At the restaurant, my throat clammed up when the food appeared and I felt awful. I was sweating and clammy. I felt so sick and I started to panic. We didn't have much money as a family and I knew the meal was costing us plenty but I couldn't eat it. I knew my father would be furious and he was. He was indignant and said he'd never take us anywhere again.

Family holidays were a nightmare for me. We'd take an annual trip to Ingoldmells on the east coast of England to stay for a week in a caravan. I'd be incredibly nervous away from home, sick to my stomach yet pretending as much as I could that everything was fine. Not content to stay in one area, it seemed my parents always wanted to explore, despite the fact that they did this every year and nothing seemed to change – Skegness, Chapel St Leonards, Mablethorpe. Mablethorpe was the worst. A meal at a pub was always part of the trip and when a huge plate of ham salad and chips was placed in front of me, I'd struggle to eat it, knowing my dad was keeping an eye on how much I was eating and mentally sighing at the waste of money. I'd scrutinise the salad to make sure it was clean, smell the ham to make sure it seemed fresh and nibble at the chips until I was sure they were thoroughly cooked. Back at the caravan, my parents would want to go out at night to see the local shows. They terrified me. They were always in pubs, which stank of booze and cigarettes. The people seemed drunk and I was shaking at the thought that someone might be sick in front of me.

I'd frequently beg to go back to the caravan on my own and on one occasion I actually said it was because I felt ill. Back at the van, I made up my bed and lay in it, shaking and shivering. I truly felt ill and was really worried that I might be sick. My parents came to check on me and I particularly remember my dad getting really cross with me, saying it was always me spoiling things for everyone and that if I wasn't better by the morning then we'd all be going home.

That was a Tuesday night. There were still three days of holiday left and I could feel the daggers in my brothers' eyes as they stared at me, muttering that I'd better be feeling better in the morning. Wednesday morning came and I forced on a smile. As always, I acted, I pretended I was all right and it started all over again, the pretence, the worrying. I kept it all to myself and didn't tell anyone because look what happened when I tried to tell people how I felt. No one understood. I felt so incredibly alone despite being surrounded by my family.

Back home, I began to relax but I started having thoughts about food. Food went into the stomach and it was the stomach that made me feel so bad. What if certain foods were upsetting it? I began restricting my diet. Vegetables tasted awful and bland so I didn't eat them. Mashed potato felt awful in my mouth and had always made me heave, so I definitely avoided that. Meat was considered okay as long as it seemed properly cooked and if it hadn't gone cold on my plate. Fruit was deemed safe, as was toast and anything that was dry and came from a packet like crisps or biscuits. I learned about food hygiene.

Our meals were basic. Back then it was mainly mash, carrots, peas and sausages, or meat and potato pie, or corned beef hash.

On Fridays we'd push the boat out and have tinned hot dog sausages in a finger roll with mustard, ketchup and fried onions. This was my best meal of the week, the one when I actually ate what was in front of me. But I soon realised that after eating I always felt so ill, so bloated. I began to find it hard to discover food that didn't make me feel ill. Weight dropped off me and in a bid to get some decent vitamins into me my parents encouraged me to swap my weekend pocket money for a bag of fruit from the market. I happily complied. I liked fruit. It didn't make me feel ill or bloated or sick, but it never lasted more than a day. I spent most times either starving hungry or feeling ill, but I actually thought this was natural for me. Neighbours and friends noticed I was losing weight. I got called 'lollipop' and 'stick'. People kept saying they'd seen more meat on a butcher's dog and that I didn't eat enough to feed a baby bird. I was pale and anaemic but no one ever bothered to test me to find out why. It was just assumed it was because I was a 'picky eater'. Their comments hurt me. Did they think I wasn't trying? I so desperately wanted to be normal and a healthy weight like all the others, but I couldn't seem to work out what the problem was.

Then one morning I woke up with stomach ache. I was 13 years old. I asked for the day off and spent the morning in bed. My parents went to work, leaving me with my middle brother. I lay in bed reading *The Two Towers* by J.R.R. Tolkien. Our hallway was being replastered and I could hear the guy making all these strange scraping noises as he sang along to his tinny little radio. The pains came and went and occasionally I'd go hot and clammy, but I didn't feel sick so it didn't cross my mind that I was about to be. I was lying down when it suddenly rushed into my throat.

I sat up fast, panicking and swallowing down hard. Sweat poured from my skin as I realised what had almost happened and I felt trapped in my little room with no air. I suddenly wanted to be downstairs and I crept down, my legs shaking and my body shivering. The carpet had been removed from the stairs and there were lumps of drying plaster on the steps. I stepped gingerly over them, feeling that I might fall at any moment and break my neck. The thought didn't scare me, but being sick did.

I crept into the front room where my brother was watching children's television, the 'Giddy Giddy Game Show'. I slumped into my dad's chair as the sunshine poured in through the window. My brother came in from the kitchen with a plate of chips he'd just cooked and the smell was awful. He'd added vinegar and salt and it was really potent. I remember the characters on the television show – Gus, Giddy, Gorilla – they were all ready to play their game. It was a Thursday. It was ten past twelve exactly. The sickness erupted again.

I rushed into the kitchen and made it to the sink. The stomach cramps were the same, the taste just as awful as I remembered and worst of all was the inability to breathe. I began to panic as the edge of my vision blackened and I knew I might pass out, but just when I thought it couldn't get any worse it stopped. I rinsed my mouth, cleaned the sink and went back into the lounge. My brother didn't say anything. He just carried on eating his chips. I became aware that some of the vomit was down the sleeve of my school shirt. I was too exhausted to clean it away, too scared to look at it. I knew my mum finished work at 1 pm. I felt better with her around. I knew that when she came back things would be better.

They weren't. She came home, heard what had happened, then went out to prune some flowers in the back garden. It was a lovely day outside and the only chance she'd have to do it. I wanted to see her, speak to her, smell her reassuring scent, but as I stood up to go outside the sickness came again, more violently this time. I didn't make it to the sink quickly enough. I was ashamed my mum had to clean it up. I was crying and desperate for all the horror to be over. She sent me back into the lounge and I wanted a drink. My mouth was so dry and there was that horrible taste. I felt like having sweet black tea, even though I'd never drunk it before.

My dad came home on his lunch break and when he heard what had happened he said the last thing I needed was tea. What would be best, he declared, was a cup of milk to line the stomach. I thought he was wrong, but he was the first aider at the swimming pool. He'd taken all these tests and examinations in health. He could restart an unbeating heart or deliver a baby if he had to so surely he must know what he was talking about? I drank the milk, then promptly sicked it up again. After that, I took no suggestions about what to have from my father. My trust in him had evaporated. How could he get it so wrong? Didn't he realise how serious it was for me?

The next day, I didn't eat or drink, nor the next, or the next. I was terrified that if I put anything into my stomach it would come up again. The little weight I had was disappearing. I was 5 feet 7 inches tall and weighed 5 stone 13 pounds. I looked a mess. I'd read of some girls being admitted into hospitals and force-fed and I didn't want that to happen to me. Images of what had happened to suffragettes on hunger strikes filled me. So I took a sip of water four days after first being ill. It stayed down. Three hours after that I asked for soup. Mum only had the vegetable variety which I didn't usually like, but I ate some and it stayed down. My stomach hurt to eat but I forced myself to do so, knowing that if I didn't I'd end up in hospital or I'd die. The fear of hospital was stronger than the fear of dying.

Every time the clock reached ten past twelve on a Thursday became a dangerous time for me. I felt that this was the time when I would get sick and I always tried to be at home just in case. It caused me trouble at school because the morning schooling didn't finish until twenty past twelve. I engineered timed trips to the school toilet just in case to protect me. No one seemed to notice and no one commented.

My sports teacher had spoken to my dad because she was worried I was anorexic. He'd asked me if I was and I said no, because I wasn't. I wanted to be fat. I would have loved to be able to pinch an inch of fat around my waist and have burgeoning curves like all the other girls.

I became so aware of others being ill that I was on constant alert and listening into people's conversations to see if they or anyone close to them had been sick. If I heard something worrying I stayed as far away from them as I could, but even so just hearing about sickness made me panic and feel so ill that invariably I would get sent home from school. I'd sit in school assemblies and if anyone left because they felt ill, I would start to feel ill as well and have to leave. If I was in class and someone started to cough violently, it would terrify me so much that I'd start to feel sick and have to leave. Sickness seemed to be everywhere. I couldn't escape from it. I was living in a permanent bubble of fear, nervous worry and panic.

Work

As the time came for me to leave school and with examinations imminent, I knew (for my family at least) that getting a job and bringing home some money was more important than getting qualifications. My dad was fond of telling anyone who'd listen that those who went to university didn't end up with good jobs. They just ended up with bad debts. So despite my intelligence I left school before taking my exams and took a job in a factory that made school uniforms. It was a youth training scheme position and I had to sit in a hot sweaty factory trying my best to get through a 37-hour week for £45. I was working just as hard as everyone else, but I couldn't stand it there. The women were so bitchy and I could hear them all talking about me: 'the thin, skinny, pale girl'.

I'd never been able to stand up for myself and in a factory full of women I wilted like a flower with no sun or water. I couldn't make it through my shifts. I'd go home for lunch and barely manage to eat a scone without feeling full and then sick, before returning to work and suffering with panics and trying not to cry in front of everyone. Eventually I told my mum I couldn't stay there so she got me a job at the factory where she worked. I thought it would be easier working in the same place as my mum. If I panicked she'd be there to soothe and comfort me. But it didn't work that way. The money was a lot better and the environment a little easier, but my emetophobia was just as bad as it had ever been.

Then I took a turn for the worse. To this day I'm not sure what caused it, but I know I was in an argument with my eldest brother and suddenly I couldn't take it any more. I was fed up with everything. I was tired of being scared, tired of struggling through each day, tired of wanting to be healthy, tired of feeling ill, tired of *life*. I was 17 years old and I just broke down. I cried and I cried, trying to tell my parents how I felt, but not knowing if they understood. Years of pain and terror poured out of me in one giant burst of hiccupping breaths.

An appointment at the doctors was made for me. I wrote a letter to the doctor, knowing I wouldn't be able to say it all over again. My doctor read the letter and asked me if I still felt that way. I did. I just wanted to end the constant fear. I just wanted to be healthy. The doctor had never heard of emetophobia. I knew I had it. I'd looked it up in a dictionary. The symptoms were mine exactly, and more. My doctor referred me to a psychotherapist and wrote me a sick note that stated I was suffering with nervous depression and signed me off work for six months. The psychotherapist came to my house and he'd never heard of emetophobia so I had to explain what it was to him. He listened, nodded reassurringly and then told me in no uncertain terms that I didn't have emetophobia. He said I was just a naturally nervous, anxious, sensitive person and I'd gotten myself into a vicious circle of anxiety.

I went to see him a second time and by then I was on some prescribed medication to lower my anxiety levels and lift my depression. I sat in his hospital room feeling quite mellow and not so distressed now that I'd told people how I felt, yet as I sat listening to him I felt that he didn't know what he was talking about. He kept mentioning anorexia and bulimia and felt certain I had one of those diseases. Was he kidding? There was no way I was going to stick a finger down the back of my throat. And I wasn't afraid of being fat. I wanted to put on weight. Why wasn't he listening? I never went back to see him. He wasn't helping. He hadn't even heard of my condition. The doctor kept prescribing tablets and signing me off sick, but nothing was done for me. I knew I had to deal with this myself and resolved to find a way. I had brains. I'd use them and work through this on my own.

I realised that I felt under more pressure with others around me. I knew I needed to work in an environment where I'd mostly be on my own, but what sort of job? I had no qualifications and jobs were scarce. Then one day I spotted an advertisement for a post working in the kiosk at a petrol station at the top of my road. It was a solitary job with people coming in and out occasionally to pay for petrol. I went for the interview and got the job and actually enjoyed it. When it wasn't busy, I could sit and write my stories, read my books, or watch television. I could make a hot drink when I needed, go to the toilet when I needed to and have my lunch break when I felt ready to eat. The mechanics next door were funny and friendly and became great friends. Bob always had the ability to make me laugh with his cheeky banter and Anthony in the car sales section was a true salesman with a lovely sense of humour.

For the first time in a long time, I seemed to fit in. At 19 years of age I'd finally found a place that I could enjoy. I had odd moments of panic and fear when I had to go home, but they were few and far between. Then shock, horror, one day someone asked me out. Steven (not his real name) seemed a real gentleman and it wasn't long before we were going out regularly. Six months into the relationship, I was offered my own council flat and Steven moved in with me. I felt like I was moving on, gaining some control over my phobia even though it was always there, ever present, lurking in the shadows, waiting to spring a surprise. When I did succumb, as frequently happened after most meals, Steven didn't have much sympathy. The relationship soured as I began to realise that he was mentally abusing me. I'd got no self-esteem again. He'd convinced me to leave the garage and go on state benefits with him, whilst he drank himself into oblivion with whisky most nights. Every time he started to drink, my stomach would churn. Would tonight be the night he threw up? I knew I wouldn't be able to handle it if he did.

After five years of being with Steven I found myself with no savings, no car, no home and no job. We were living in a field in a caravan which had no hot water and no toilet. We had to walk a hundred yards to the nearest one. My emetophobia had gone into overdrive and the weight was dropping off me each week. I was either ill, crying or depressed. I caught the flu and lay in bed, hardly able to breathe and without an appetite. Strangely, I realised that now I wasn't eating any food my stomach actually felt fine. Odd, but I never thought to mention it to anyone. I'd spent so many years being like this that I thought it was just me.

My parents came to visit, saw the state I was in and refused to go home without me. Steven was out, cadging booze money from his mum, so I went. I had no fight and I would have resisted if I had. The doctor came and said I was close to hospitalisation. I had bronchitis as well as flu. He prescribed some antibiotics. I recovered from the flu but as soon as I started eating again my stomach got bad. My emetophobia was ever present. I was just so nervous all the time. When would I not feel sick? I hardly slept because I'd dream of being sick and wake up expecting to do so. I'd spend the days hiding away from people in case they were ill and I didn't want to catch anything. I'd certainly sworn off from men.

Marriage

Then, just after I'd started a new job in a shop, I met my future husband. I told him about my emetophobia and he understood that I got panicky. He sympathised and tried his best to calm me down. When the panic attacks were at full throttle he'd ask me what he could do to help. I didn't have any answers. I didn't know anyone else like me, who suffered like me. How could he help me? Even doctors didn't seem to know what to do.

As our wedding day drew closer, I wondered how I'd cope. Like any little girl I'd dreamed of a huge white wedding in a beautiful church, but these ceremonies took time. What if I felt sick during the service? I could hardly escape the way I usually would by running to a quiet room and being on my own. My fiancé would think I was jilting him or something. I decided that the fear also came from my worry about lack of control, so surely if I controlled the day as much as I could then I might be able to get through it without humiliating myself and upsetting my future groom.

On the day, everything went according to plan. I could barely get toast down my throat first thing in the morning. It felt all clammed up and the food kept getting stuck. But I pushed on, forcing it down, knowing that if I were to be sick then it would be better to do so with food in my stomach. The hairdresser came to the house and arranged my hair, make-up and veil. Then I dressed while sipping black coffee (a drink I've found helps my stomach when it's churning over) with my mother's warning ringing in my ears not to spill it over my dress. The video man and photographer arrived and strangely enough I was kept so busy being told how to sit, how to position my bouquet, when to smile, and so on that I forgot how nervous I was. When the time came for me to go to the church I was actually very calm.

There was a slight delay because the organist had not turned up but another was quickly volunteered and I glided into church feeling serene and calm, amazed at how I felt. Afterwards, all the adrenalin and tension in my body came pouring out and by nine o'clock that evening I just knew I couldn't go on. Physically, I was shattered. My husband and I retired to the bridal suite and I was able to remove my veil and heavy dress and the 'act' I'd been putting on through the day. All I could think of was how tired I was and that the next day we were going to have to make a four-hour drive to our honeymoon destination. How would I be on the trip?

After many months of marriage my husband suggested I try hypnotherapy. We'd both heard that lots of people had had their phobias cured in this way. I decided to give it a go. A lady came to the house. She 'hypnotised' me, though I'll state categorically that I was just sitting on the couch with my eyes closed and wasn't hypnotised at all, while she gave me various suggestions. I did what I was told and performed my meditation 'homework' every night before bed, but I wasn't cured. I was still terrified, facing each day like I was running a merciless gauntlet of trials and tests.

Behind the fear was the knowledge that both of us wanted children and the one thing stopping me was the fear of morning sickness. How could I inflict such a thing on myself? How could I go into one of my panics if I was pregnant? What sort of risk would I be putting a baby under, feeling like that? The poor thing would get hooked on adrenalin or something. I so desperately wanted to have my husband's child. A son would be perfect, but did I dare?

Children

I put a great deal of thought into it and eventually (it must have been a good day) I decided that I wanted a child more than I feared being sick. Our first attempt resulted in a six-week miscarriage that devastated me, but I wanted to try again. I'd not felt sick during the brief part of pregnancy I'd experienced so decided it was worth the risk. I got pregnant again nine months later and the morning sickness was awful.

I'd never experienced symptoms of nausea like it. It was mixed with pangs of hunger and I didn't know what to do. I nibbled on bananas and barley-sugar sweets to settle my stomach and quickly realised that if I forced myself to eat the sickness would abate for about thirty minutes, but I was terrified I'd actually throw up. After two days of it I burst into tears and begged my husband to call my mum. I wanted her with me so badly and I was convinced that if she came the sickness would miraculously disappear. Idiot thinking – but you never tire of needing your mum, no matter what your age.

Mum drove three hours to be with me and offered to stay for a week, but she told me in no uncertain terms that I was grown up now and about to be a mother so I had to start dealing with my fear. Start? What did they think I'd been doing for years? I dealt with it every day. Everyone decided that the best thing for me was not to let me hide in my room and so they forced me out on every occasion. I'd cram my bag with snacky things and drinks so that if the nausea started I'd have rescue supplies. I was so scared, so nervous, constantly on the look-out for toilets. If I was somewhere that didn't have a public bathroom I'd look around and think 'Okay, if I'm sick, I'll go over there, that'll hide me.'

After ten weeks, the nausea disappeared and I sighed the biggest sigh of relief. I actually felt a little more like my old self, though I'd still feel ill after eating, but, hey, that was me. The pregnancy went well and at 41 weeks I was induced. I had questioned the midwives on the side effects of the prostaglandin pessary and allowed them to use it. Then I waited. Eleven hours later my son was born. As he struggled to breathe his first breath I felt hot and dizzy. I wanted a black coffee. I wanted everyone in the room to leave me alone with my husband and son. When they handed me my baby I cried with joy, but also wept at how ill I felt. Nothing had changed.

For some reason I'd thought that, just maybe, I'd be different as a mother. That with someone else so utterly reliant on me, so dependent on me, I'd forget all my own worries and just think of my husband and son. But it didn't work that way. I was able to cope whenever my son sicked up milk. It was just milk after all, it wasn't like he had a virus, but then he got gastroenteritis just days after starting at nursery at eight months of age. I couldn't deal with it at all. My husband was at work and all I wanted to do was run screaming into the garden. I had to clean him up, touch the sicked-on clothes while trying not to breathe in and chuck them in the washing machine. I had to mop the floor and disinfect it and then cuddle my screaming, ill child. I didn't want to hold him. I feared him. What if he passed his illness on to me? What if I got sick? I was terrified, almost frozen with fear and uncertainty. Beneath all of that, there was self-loathing for not being able to soothe an ill child, for not holding him as close to me as I could, for not kissing him better. I felt guilty, cowardly and ashamed. I hated myself. How could I be like this? Why couldn't I be a normal mum?

It didn't help that by this time I was pregnant again and once more feeling ill. I felt surrounded by sickness and nausea, attacked from all angles. I was bigger, heavier and more tired and I was expecting twins. They say that sickness can be worse with twins, but actually I thought it was better than before. The morning sickness lasted about a week and then was gone. The twins were born at 37 weeks, despite numerous hospital admissions in premature labour from 26 weeks gestation and uncountable doses of steroids for their lungs. I'd been to three different hospitals in London for a week at a time to stop the labour and each stay was spent in a void of fear. Germs were everywhere in hospitals – all those sick people. I was unbelieveably glad to be free from the threat. I had an elective caesarean section, counting the marks on the ceiling as a way of focusing on something other than the knowledge that I couldn't get up and run away. I'd been incredibly aware that the anaesthetist had a few cardboard sick bowls next to her because a lot of women are sick during the procedure. I kept repeating my mantra, 'Please don't let it be me, please don't let it be me.'

You would have thought I'd be thinking about the babies like a normal expectant mother, and I did when they were born and I heard them cry straight away. I burst into tears myself and couldn't wait to hold them. This is how emetophobia gets you. Three years later, I went on to get pregnant again. It wasn't planned but I was still excited. I wasn't so anxious about being sick this time because I knew I'd gotten through a twin pregnancy without being ill and figured I'd be okay again. I was. My four children are now aged seven, six and three.

Mostly I cope quite normally through the day, forcing myself to do things that other emets wouldn't, just because I know I have no choice. I baulk at journeys, trips away from home, any suggestion that I need to go into a doctor's surgery, but I pretty much cope, unless I feel ill or my kids catch something. Then I'm hopeless. When the panic attacks set in they are worse than they've ever been before, but at least they're less frequent and to most people I'm normal. I'm a loving mother and I adore my kids, but that doesn't stop me from feeling scared silly when they get sick – only I'm scared for me, not them.

Recently I noticed the same behaviour patterns developing in my eldest son. The health visitor referred him to a counsellor and he's currently getting help. Will it work? I have my doubts, but what can I do? I don't want him to suffer like me or all the other emets I know. I worry that I've passed the fear on, though I feel sure I've always hidden it from them. Wouldn't my other children have it too? Thankfully they don't.

I have also been diagnosed with coeliac disease, which goes some way to explain why I have spent so much of my life feeling sick after eating. My body couldn't cope with the gluten in the food. I was losing so much weight because of the malabsorption of food, not because I was being a 'picky eater', which is what everyone thought. I have feelings of resentment about not having it diagnosed while I was a child (a simple blood test).

Then I might not have spent so much time feeling sick. Maybe the fear wouldn't have got such a grip on me if I hadn't spent so much time suffering and reliving the possibility of the swimming pool event?

My health is better now that I have a gluten-free diet, but the fear has not lessened. Thirty years on, I'm still suffering in spite of having tried lots of different ways to relieve it. I still have my little 'mad thoughts' as I call them. I know they're illogical.

I know I'm overreacting about something that people do every day, but that doesn't help; nothing seems to. I've just had to find strategies to deal with it all.

CHAPTER THREE

Emetophobia as a Catalyst

Emetophobia itself is bad enough, but what if it becomes something more? What if it has such a grip on your life and thoughts throughout the day that you find it triggers something else? When this happens, you might not even be aware of it. It just seems like one more thing rolled into the whole terrifying aspect that is the emetophobia. You can see why you feel that way, but others on the outside looking in don't know because they can't read your thoughts unless you tell them what is happening:

> I stopped going out after a while. Going places was just too much. I was constantly on the look-out for ill people. I feared all the germs I might be exposing myself to and I hated being surrounded by lots of people. All that busyness. All that bustling, toing and fro-ing. I'd feel trapped. (Dina, 21)

Dina hits on the most salient points of the problem quite clearly.

Phobias

For those already suffering from emetophobia, no matter which type of sufferer they purport to be, developing another sort of phobia, one created and stemming from the original emetophobia, seems to be something they are resigned to.

Survey results show that 34 per cent of emetophobic sufferers also have agoraphobia.[1] Agoraphobia is assumed by many to be a fear of open spaces, but it is actually a fear of public places. What's the difference, I hear you ask? Well, a fear of public places means that the fear is centred on the possibility of contact with other people, whereas a fear of open spaces means there is less chance of physical contact with another person and it is the *space* that is central to the fear, rather than the proximity of people.

The emets that reported being mildly agoraphobic also reported some discomfort when they had to walk any distance. This discomfort manifested itself in feelings of unsteadiness, being off balance and/or a sensation of the path beneath their feet moving and tilting whilst the buildings and surroundings appeared to move and converge along their peripheral vision. These sensations induced physical symptoms of nausea, which in turn, because of the emetophobia, triggered panic attacks. (Reading these results, it appeared to this author that the symptoms were strangely similar to those of travel sickness.)

For many years doctors have insisted that phobic problems in their patients were all 'in the mind' and a lot of emets reported being dismissed by their GPs with endless prescriptions for antidepressants (which themselves had side effects including nausea, so were not taken).

In October 1997, Gut Reaction reported on how one agoraphobe experiencing such symptoms improved considerably after having his underlying inappropriate childhood reflexes corrected. These underlying reflexes and balance tests were undertaken by a research college in London. In total there were six tests and the patients tested were informed that they could choose to stop the testing at any time. In between each test

1 Dean, L. (1998) *Survey of Emetophobia Sufferers.* Gut Reaction. Available at www.gut-reaction.freeserve.co.uk/survey-results.htm. Reprinted with permission.

their anxiety levels were rated on a scale of one to ten. The tests were as follows:

1. Patients had to stand on two footplates in front of a canvas wall which had a side panel attached either side of the patient. A harness was fitted for safety so the patient would not fall during the test. The patient was instructed to stare straight ahead whilst the canvas wall was moved forwards and backwards and the side panels also moved from side to side. The footplates would then be tilted slightly whilst the patient attempted to maintain balance.

2. Eardrum pressure was measured by fitting a small rubber earpiece inside the ear and applying pressure.

3. A hearing test was performed in a soundproof room. Patients had to press a buzzer every time they heard a tone through the headphones and the results were plotted to form an audiograph.

4. Patients were sat in a chair with electrodes attached above and either side of each eye. These electrodes were to measure eye movements. Patients had to follow a red light being moved across a screen in front of them and they were not permitted to move their heads.

5. A black and white striped curtain was enclosed around the patient to form a cylinder and then the cylinder revolved from right to left. Lights were then turned out and the procedure repeated as the chair the patient was in was spun gently.

6. The last test was the most notorious. Water of 42 degrees and 32 degrees celcius (above and below body temperature) was poured into the ear canal and the patient's eyes monitored for nystagmus (flickering).

> (This action stimulates the balance system and can actually lead to vomiting.)[2]

These tests would then prove whether a patient had a *postural* dysfunction or a *middle ear* dysfunction. However, the results were not always immediately apparent unless the patient became acutely distressed. (These tests may go some way to explain why some emetophobes have balance problems in childhood which suddenly become more acute and noticeable in adult life when we are more aware of our phobia.)

When the test results were compared against a control group (those without any dizziness or panic problems), the eye movement test results were usually similar. Yet in contrast, the postural sway test results showed that patients suffering with panic attacks and agoraphobia were undeniably less stable than the control group, particularly in the cylinder tests.

Early research suggests that patients with agoraphobia and dizziness do have balance problems. These should be checked out and if necessary investigated by their doctors and treated. Treatment consists of manipulative exercise, such as that proposed by the Institute for Neuro-Physiological Psychology (INPP) (see Organisations and online resources, p.156).

Other phobias reported by emetophobes were fear of insects, claustrophobia, social phobia and obsessive compulsive disorders (OCDs) which were mainly to do with the need to wash their hands and bodies and keep from being contaminated by germs and bacteria. Contaminants were mainly seen as coming from other people and 'things'. These undisclosed 'things' could be anything, such as library books, clothes, animals, pets, flowers, cars, seats and toilets. Just the act of touching something was a constant worry. Emetophobia sufferers have no idea of the history of an object. They do not know if it has been touched or

---

2 Dean, L. (1997) *Neuro-Physiological Psychology*. Gut Reaction. Available at www.gut-reaction.freeserve.co.uk/neuro-physio.htm. Reprinted with permission.

played with by someone suffering with a stomach virus, nor do they know where it has been. The risk is unknown, but in an emet's mind the risk is great. As their unofficial motto seems to be 'Better to be safe than sorry,' they wash themselves and their hands constantly, some doing this so often that their skin cracks and dries out, leaving their hands painfully useless.

These OCDs can also develop into 'rituals' that the sufferers feel they must go through each night, otherwise they will get sick. One sufferer reported that she had a special pair of washable slippers that she kept for her nightly walk from the shower to her bed. These slippers were not used around the rest of the house. Each night she would shower and then dry with a freshly laundered towel. Once dry, she would step into these 'clean' slippers and walk to her bed which had fresh sheets every day. In that way and that way only would she feel safe enough to sleep.

When questioned as to why she felt the need to be so clean and hygienic at night-time, she replied that the last time she got sick was at night. For some reason, she'd got it into her head that maybe the bed had been contaminated by bacteria and she'd breathed it in. This way, with fresh sheets, a clean body and feet that hadn't touched the floor, she felt she could sleep easier in her bed.

Anxiety in emetophobic sufferers should never be underestimated. It can become so powerful that an observer might sometimes see them physically shaking or trembling. Peter Blythe of the INPP explains anxiety:

> Anxiety is experienced in three ways: cognitively (in a person's thoughts), somatically (in physiological and biological actions) and feelings. Many approaches to treating anxiety focus on the cognitive and behavioural aspects, by attempting to alter attitudes and actions to anxiety-producing situations.
>
> [Some anxiety] is so acute that feelings overwhelm any attempt by higher (cognitive) centres in the brain to

> control them. Somatic changes such as shallow breathing, dry mouth, cold hands and feet, tightness in the chest, sinking in the stomach, rapid pulse, light-headedness, dizziness and muscular tenseness occur with such intensity that the individual ceases to be in control of their actions; temporary loss of cortical control is experienced as disorientation and in some cases, panic. ...
>
> Blythe found that adults who...failed to respond to the various therapies of choice, despite a real desire to get better, all showed signs of neurological dysfunction related to immature reflexes which included problems with balance, co-ordination, perceptual skills and the functioning of the sympathetic division of the autonomic nervous system – the part of the nervous system responsible for involuntary responses, particularly to danger. This heightened arousal, in turn, can result in the experience of greater fear, fear of fear in future (anticipatory anxiety) and adaptive behaviours which are inappropriate to the situation from an objective standpoint, such as avoidance, frustration, anger and sometimes depression.[3]

Depression is a common symptom amongst emetophobes, occurring in 73 per cent of respondents. Of this 73 per cent, 31 per cent had felt suicidal.[4]

Claustrophobia was experienced by 13 per cent of respondents. This claustrophobia could be experienced in two different ways. First, the claustrophobia could occur because of their fear of being enclosed in a small space, which most people understand claustrophobia to be. Second, the claustrophobia came from a sort of 'internal' fear of being enclosed. Emetophobes experience panic or symptoms of feeling ill, then feel trapped

---

3 Blythe, P. (2002–2006) *Neurodevelopmental Delay in Adults.* Chester: INPP. Available at www.inpp.org.uk/INPP_3_5_NDD_adults2.php. Reprinted with permission.

4 Dean, L. (1998) *Survey of Emetophobia Sufferers.* Gut Reaction. Available at www.gut-reaction.freeserve.co.uk/survey-results.htm. Reprinted with permission.

inside of their own body, unable to escape the sensations of nausea and sickness they are experiencing. They are enclosed in the small space of their own body and when these symptoms of panic are experienced, most emetophobes feel better by standing outside and breathing fresh air, or going to a large open area or garden.

Emetophobia itself is a powerful fear and, as we have read, it can trigger many other fears, OCDs, anxiety and depression. Not all emetophobes will experience other phobias or uncontrollable thoughts or obsessions, but some will. The onus is on the emetophobes to try to speak out and break the silence; to let others know how they are feeling and why. Family members, teachers, doctors and therapists can only do so much if they don't know the truth. How can anyone help, if they don't know what is wrong?

CHAPTER FOUR

Worklife?

The question emetophobes have to ask themselves when they become old enough to go out and work is: 'Will I be able to do it?' The majority of people think nothing of getting up and going to work. They wake, shower, dress and travel to wherever they have to go, work their shift, travel home and then do it all again the next day, five, sometimes six days a week, depending on the job. But for emetophobes, it just isn't that simple. The very first thing that pops into their head the second they wake up is 'How do I feel?' They will lie for a moment, analysing their health, before getting up. If there is anything that signifies something isn't right, then in most probability they will not go out that day and will spend the day in a constant turmoil of anxiety. Yet even if they wake and feel fine, they will still spend the day in this state of anxiety and nervous tension.

Why? Because there are so many risks to an emet in going out and mixing with all those people: people who may have been in contact with a sick child or relative; people who may have struggled into work themselves feeling ill but determined to get through the day, unaware of the terror they are inflicting upon their emet colleague by just being there; people who may have been drinking; people who may be sick at work; people who may bring germs and viruses into the workplace.

The inability to control who enters the work environment is a huge source of stress and panic to an emetophobe. Personally, I can recall a day before I got signed off from work when a colleague who sat next to me at the factory had been out the night before, crawling all the pubs and bars. Her face was as pale as snow and she had shadows beneath her eyes. As soon as I noticed how ill she looked, I just had to know why she looked so bad. When she told me why and I realised she had a hangover I relaxed a little, knowing it wasn't something I could catch, but I still needed to know how she felt. Did she feel sick? Had she been sick? Was she nauseated?

She had no idea of my emetophobia so didn't realise the importance of her answer when she said that her stomach and head felt like a washing machine on the spin cycle. I panicked. Instantly my own heart rate went up. I went clammy, my mouth was dry and my palms were sweaty. My eyes flickered and a nerve beneath one began to twitch. I felt sick. I was going into a panic and the adrenalin flooding my system screamed at me to run and get away from the source of the danger – the possibility that she might be sick.

I kept shifting in my seat, trying to concentrate on my work, watching the clock, desperate for hometime, but I'd only just got there. It was morning and there were still eight hours to go. I knew I wouldn't last it out. Every sound my friend made, clearing her throat or coughing, had me nearly jumping out of my seat and gasping in fear. I kept checking her, asking her how she felt. She must have thought how kind I was to be worrying about her health.

When it got to lunch break and I'd questioned my friend on how she was after every trip to the factory toilet, my throat was so clammed up with fear and my stomach so twisted in nausea and terror that I couldn't eat a thing. I burst into tears and when asked what was wrong all I could say was that I felt so ill. I was only 17 then and one of the older ladies went to tell the supervisor I was feeling ill and had to go home for the afternoon. As far as I'm aware, my colleague was never sick and she went out drinking again the next night, leaving me totally confused as to why she would want to do that to herself.

This can be a typical reaction for an emetophobe and the reactions of phobics can be a lot more pronounced if their colleague isn't drunk but actually sickening for something or has an ill child. How to spot an emet? Emets will always enquire as to the exact nature of your child's illness and whether he or she was actually vomiting. Subsequent questioning may be about whether the child ate something odd or how many times he or she vomited. Emets will not be content with someone's vague comment about his or her child being ill. They need the details. It's almost a voyeuristic tendency.

They are terrified of sickness and vomiting but feel compelled to know about it. They have to look at someone bending down to know if they're vomiting or not. They have to look at people parked by the roadside to see if someone is being sick. They cannot tear their eyes away until they see that the people are fine. Even if those people are fine, they will still tremble and panic a little at the possibility. Thoughts about 'What would I have done if I had seen them being sick?' will play over and over in their minds, making them numb with fear until they can make themselves focus on something else.

This is how emets get through the day at work. They intensely focus their mind on other things so that they cannot think about illness or sickness or contamination. Emetophobes can actually be very hard workers because they work so intensely in order to keep their thoughts occupied by something else. If they're concentrating on their work then they're not listening to nearby conversations about who feels ill or who had a stomach bug last week.

In the survey, 70 per cent of respondents said that they were employed in some fashion, but few had actually told their work colleagues of their phobia. Of respondents 80 per cent fear vomiting in public, so when they get ill at work, whether this is through panic association or not, they go home, because home is safer than work. At home they can relax somewhat and the pressure of having all those people around them is off.

Because of the phobia, most emets have only part-time jobs, work from home, or are not employed at all. One emet I spoke to said that she'd been on incapacity benefit since school because she just couldn't face being at work each day. She'd tried and failed. The pressure had been too much and she'd almost had a nervous breakdown. She was on antidepressants from her doctor, but was so depressed and upset as well as being embarrassed at having to be on benefits that she was thinking of ending it all. Thankfully she did not. With help from myself, her boyfriend, doctor and family, she was encouraged to think about her life from a different perspective. She saw that even though she was effectively stuck at home, afraid of going out the door, she could still improve her life. She is now studying for a degree with the Open University and hopes that by the time she passes she will feel stronger within herself and may be able to go outside.

All of this may seem so strange to someone without emetophobia. Descriptions of such lives may seem almost unbelievable or even a little crazy. But isn't that what they are? Phobias are illogical. Sufferers know they're illogical. Take an arachnophobe, for example – someone who's terrified of spiders, a teensy little spider that can do no one any harm. The spider is probably more scared of a human being. But arachnophobes can't help their fear. They see a spider, they scream, they run, they squirm, lifting their legs off the floor if they can. They can't even look at it, but they have to see it to know that it's gone. Then when the spider has been disposed of they can relax. Only with emetophobia there is no relaxing. No one can remove the sickness for a sufferer.

CHAPTER FIVE

Relationships

Thankfully, most emetophobes are in good, secure, understanding relationships with a significant other. Twenty-one percent of respondents had told their partner about their emetophobia, but those who had not, experienced a lot of intimacy issues which were currently causing problems within their relationships, or had previously ended them.

Many emetophobes are quite knowledgeable about sickness, germs and hygiene. In the search to protect themselves, they look for information that they hope will help them. For most people it is simply good sense to keep everything clean and maintain standards of personal hygiene, but for an emetophobe, this knowledge of germs, contamination and how bacteria are passed on can be a double-edged sword when it comes to intimate relationships.

Intimacy

Take, for example, the mouth. A human mouth, like any other part of the body, contains a lot of bacteria. Saliva is in there trying to keep everything clean and of course we all brush our teeth and/or use mouthwash each day, but still there are germs inside, naturally occurring and foreign. Some emetophobes fear kissing another person because of the risk of catching some unknown germ. If a kiss is used as a greeting to friends or family members, some emetophobes report that after kissing someone they go to the bathroom and scrub at their mouths and then won't eat for a few hours in case a missed germ gets trapped on some food and passes into the stomach.

Kissing someone intimately can be a huge no-go area. One emetophobe reported that she had never had a boyfriend or relationship because she just cannot bring herself to kiss them. As soon as a man tries to get close to her by holding her hand or putting his arm around her shoulders, she just backs off. Her feelings of shame, embarrassment and fear were so great that she has now given up on ever trying to have a relationship. She is just 22 years old. When asked why she didn't just tell the person about her fear, she answered as most emets do, 'They wouldn't understand. No one does.'

Fortunately, most emets do not fear kissing their partners, but some do worry about their partner's hygiene levels, or who they might have come into contact with. The most common problem that came to fore in my research for this book was the majority of female emetophobes who felt under pressure to have children. Almost all of them want to have children themselves and find themselves dreaming about it on a daily basis, but over half admitted that they felt terrified of getting pregnant because of the possibility of morning sickness. A couple of respondents replied that they would refuse to get pregnant, even if it meant the demise of their relationship.

Pregnancy

Apart from being knowledgeable about germs and hygiene, female emets in particular are very knowledgeable about pregnancy and birth. They know exactly what can happen to them and when in regard to the possibility of sickness and vomiting.

Like most emets, I always have a stock of Motilium tablets to take in case I get really ill. I always try my hardest not to take them and a standard pack of ten tablets will usually last me well over a year. But when it came to getting pregnant, I knew that if I felt sick there wouldn't be any tablet I could take to help me. I felt able to take on that risk, especially after having had one pregnancy and knowing how well I'd actually been, but a lot of female emets will not take the risk. Their baby will be their foremost concern and as it is usually recommended not to take most medications during pregnancy they will not want to chance damaging the baby. One respondent replied that she didn't know how brave she would be able to be if she got sick. Her intention would be to stay medication free, but what if the phobia got the better of her?

Morning sickness was not the only worry. A lot of women can get sick just before labour starts and during transition (when the cervix has reached ten centimetres and they are ready to push the baby out). For this reason, a lot of female emets had previously requested caesarean sections, though this procedure also involved certain dangers. Many emets worry about the effect their emetophobia will have on their nearest and dearest. If a female emet were to have children, how would the partner feel when the mother of their children got terrified whenever their child or children got a tummy bug?

Telling someone

Most emetophobes have a generalised fear of actually telling someone that they have this fear. One lady on the forum of the International Emetophobia Society (IES; see Organisations and online resources, p.158) stated that she hadn't even known her fear had a name for years, so how could she have told someone what it was, when she didn't know herself? She also found that the way people responded on being told was not particularly encouraging. On telling a significant relation/friend/spouse, emets have reported these replies:

- Really? (in disgust)
- Well, no one likes being sick.
- Oh, I was like that once. I'm fine now. (dismissive)

- Emetophobia? What's that?
- Don't be ridiculous!

The general consensus was that when an emetophobe told another person about the fear, the majority reacted either with disbelief, disgust or were generally dismissive.

Emetophobes weigh up the pros and cons of telling another person about their emetophobia and think about the implications of doing so for a very long time. If they are telling their spouse, they tend to hope their partner will be sympathetic and kind, perhaps even ask a few questions about the phobia to help clarify just exactly how it affects the sufferer and what they could possibly do to help.

My own experiences of telling people about my own emetophobia have also been varied. My parents were sympathetic and kind, even though at the beginning they didn't fully understand the extent to which it affected me. My husband was fantastic and very supportive. Some 'friends' have looked at me as if I was telling them I'd just come out of a mental institution (or possibly needed to be in one!), whilst others have reacted with some sympathy and understanding, asking questions about it, including some of my work colleagues. If you are an emetophobic sufferer who works, I personally feel it is best to tell a few select work colleagues. Then if you have people who know how you are going to react to things they will generally try to protect you as much as they can. Though again, depending upon how phobic you are, this also can be a double-edged sword:

> I'm very open about my phobia now and it's good that people know how I feel, though sometimes I wonder about if people have been ill because they won't tell me and I never know how much I ought to avoid them. (Jackie, 43)

As you can clearly see, emetophobes never relax about the possibility of contamination, but they hide it very well.

CHAPTER SIX

The Home Environment

Not all emetophobes feel the need to confine themselves to their homes, but many do. For those emetophobes who also suffer with social phobia or claustrophobia, their home literally becomes their own prison. Because it is the only place where they feel safe and over which they feel they have control, an emetophobe can very quickly become an obsessive cleanaholic. These emetophobes also usually border on the line of depression and have OCDs:

> I clean and clean and clean. All day long. Everything gets cleaned with bleach, my floors, my surfaces, door handles, switches, anything that gets touched. I don't have carpets, just wooden floors that I can sweep and mop each day. I wash down my skirting boards and dado rails every day, my toilet and bathroom...well! I clean it every time I use it. Not just the loo seat and handles, but the floor, the shelves, the walls, everything. I can't relax. I know the germs are there and I don't want to get sick. (Kelly, 19)

One respondent reported that she sprayed every item that came in from a shop with antibacterial spray 'because you don't know who's touched it' before placing it in her bleached kitchen cupboards.[1]

It's not just the house that gets physically spritzed each time something new enters it. Some emetophobes have some very determined personal hygiene rules before they allow themselves out of the bathroom each morning and into the rest of the house. One respondent reported that she would have to clean her teeth first, taking exactly five minutes and making sure she scrubbed at her tongue as well. Then she would floss, wearing latex gloves so her hands didn't contaminate the floss about to go into her mouth. The gloves would be taken off and her hands washed before she put on another pair to wash her face with a facial scrub. These gloves would then be discarded and her hands washed again before she picked up a clean flannel to wash her ears and neck. Next, she would pick up her comb (soaked each night in bleach) and comb her hair, laying it on the flannel she'd used, so both these items could be placed in the sink afterwards to soak. She would then don another pair of gloves to apply her make-up (but not lipstick because of the germs she could put near her mouth). Next she had a special robe and slippers to wear to get her to the bedroom to get dressed. Fresh clothes were worn every day and the previous day's clothes would be gathered and taken to the laundry in her utility room, where she would wash her hands again. This sufferer washed her hands so many times a day that the skin around her knuckles and between the fingers was cracked and often bled. Her skin was scaly and felt raw and she confided that she easily could get through a whole tube of antiseptic cream in a single week.

Of course not all emetophobes are like this, though most will keep their homes as clean as they can. But then what about items

---

1 Dean, L. (1998) *Survey of Emetophobia Sufferers.* Gut Reaction. Available at www.gut-reaction.freeserve.co.uk/survey-results.htm. Reprinted with permission.

or people that might need access to an emetophobe's home? Most people wouldn't blink if you asked them to remove their shoes before entering a home, but what if you asked them to clean their hands with antiseptic wash before stepping over the threshold? Sufferers have reported feeling so uncomfortable at having outside guests inside their homes. They have plastic covers over the chairs for the guests to sit on while they sit on a separate chair.

It is fair to say that paranoia plays a large part in emetophobia, not so much on the understanding that someone is out to get you, rather that something is out to get you – and that something is a sickness bug. Sufferers know that a virus or bacteria are not seeking them out, but they often feel their lives are a constant battle to avoid them, no matter what the situation. Some emetophobic sufferers are registered with their doctors as suffering from agoraphobia. They have carers coming to their homes to bring them shopping or books from the library, perhaps also cleaning for them or hanging out the washing. These sufferers know that as soon as their carers leave they will systematically go around the house cleaning everything that the carer has touched:

> I watch her the second she comes into my house. I try to keep her in one area so that I don't have so much to clean afterwards, because I'm so tired. I'm so tired of this battle against bacteria. The fear of them. I can remember when I was smaller, cutting open apples and leaving them on the side to see if they'd turn brown in my bedroom. If they did, I'd clean my room some more. It was an endless cycle. I had no idea that the apple would *always* turn brown. (Hillary, 31)

CHAPTER SEVEN

Illness

When sufferers tell a doctor that they think they have emetophobia (assuming the doctor has heard of emetophobia), the immediate assumption is often that the affliction only affects the sufferer when he or she has a virus or feels unwell for some other reason. It is a common misconception that the occurrence of emetophobia is limited to when emetophobes are exposed to the subject of their fear. As you have been reading so far, this phobia can affect suffers every second of every day, and one of the worst ways in which it can affect them is when it comes to medical matters.

Perhaps you imagine that an emetophobe would not be afraid of being at a doctor's surgery; that the phobic sufferer would welcome the advice and help of someone medically trained. Well yes, they do appreciate the help but actually going into a doctor's surgery is extremely difficult. The very idea of actually entering the practice and sitting down and waiting for what might be a long time in a room that is and has been filled with sick people can fill emetophobes with such dread that they will do anything to avoid it. They know that *anyone* with *anything* could have been in that waiting room. It doesn't matter that logically on that particular day the surgery has only held people with coughs and sniffles; the fact is that sufferers have no idea if someone with a sickness bug or virus has been in there or whether that bug is virulent or highly contagious. They will instinctively feel that the risk of going into the surgery is too high, even if they have shooting pains down their left arm and are experiencing all the symptoms of a possible heart attack. The fear of having a cardiac infarction will not be as great as the fear of going into that surgery and catching what to everyone else would just be a simple stomach bug. This may seem an extreme example, as if I am trying to exaggerate the control of the phobia over a sufferer, but I am not. Quite simply, to an emetophobe the fear of death is nothing compared to the fear of being sick and vomiting.

Many years ago, when I first decided to write this book, I asked emetophobes to contact me with their story via a forum's message board. One lady's story really struck a chord with me and to this day I have wondered how I myself might react (though I hope I will never have to find out). This lady was in her fifties but had been emetophobic for many years. She told most people about her fear, assuming that it was best for people to know why she might react in certain ways in certain situations and this usually worked well for her until the day she discovered a lump in her breast. She tried to ignore it, hoping it would go away, but knowing what it might signify and that at some point she might have to go and see a doctor about it. She told her husband, who badgered her to go, but she just knew she couldn't go into a doctor's surgery. Her husband told her to sit in the car while he sat in the waiting room and he'd fetch her when her name was called.

She duly waited and when her husband came to get her she held her breath to walk through the room where all the sick people sat. She'd been berating herself in the car for putting herself through this, assuming that the doctor would tell her it was a simple cyst; that she was threatening her health by being in the doctor's consultation room. She can remember eyeing the sink, knowing that if she was sick she could run to it, that she was probably in the best place if she were to be ill, but none of this did anything to calm her down. She had a massive panic attack and her husband had to tell the doctor why.

She was examined and the doctor referred her to the hospital. The sufferer was more concerned about catching a germ in hospital than she was about having cancer. Her results and biopsy were positive for a very aggressive form of breast cancer. The only thought going through her head was not that she could die but rather that she would be forced to have chemotherapy and she might vomit. The possibility of this overwhelmed her so much that she had a breakdown. The medical staff involved believed that it was caused by the diagnosis rather than for anything else. Indeed, they couldn't understand that anything else could be a consideration at that time.

This sufferer and her very supportive husband had to tell the nurses what was going on and in every case of meeting a new nurse, a new doctor, a new consultant, not a single person had heard of emetophobia. It had to be explained yet again. The sufferer had to state repeatedly why she was so scared and why she did not want treatment. When the staff finally understood, the sufferer was offered the chance of anti-emetic medication and it took over three weeks of deliberation before she accepted that this would be what she would have to do if she wanted to live. And she did want to live, just not in that way.

She underwent a radical mastectomy which left her with a lot of scarring. Her lymph nodes were also removed for testing. She underwent chemotherapy and radiation therapy and took her anti-sickness pills. She felt very nauseous but did not vomit and her only thought throughout every second spent in hospital was not that she was fighting cancer but the fact that she was fighting being sick and vomiting over the floor. At home she'd linger in bed and concentrate on not being sick. She won her battle against cancer and I'm so very proud of her bravery and determination to go through with her treatment, despite her terror. But has the experience helped her fear of being at a doctor's surgery? No, she still sits outside in the car and waits for her husband to collect her. She still holds her breath going through the waiting room. She still fears being sick. She has had counselling throughout her cancer treatment and says that even though she could sit with someone and rationally see that her phobia was not as bad as cancer, she still felt that if she got cancer again her fear of the side effects of chemotherapy would be greater than the fear of her illness.

This knowledge is something that doctors need to understand when an emetophobic sufferer sits before them and tells them about his or her fear. As you can see, a lot of the fear that arises from emetophobia comes not just from what the sufferer knows about germs and sickness in general, but also from the unknown and the unseen. Germs, viruses and bacteria are not visible to the human eye. Emetophobic sufferers have no idea whether the surface they are touching is infected or not, so generally they opt to believe that it is and take precautions such as hand-washing or not eating. A doctor's surgery, consulting room or hospital are considered high-risk areas by emetophobes, not only because of what they might contract via infection but also because of what they might see.

Doctors

Despite the fear of vomiting and sickness, whether of themselves vomiting or others doing so, an emetophobic sufferer feels compelled to make sure that others are okay and not being sick. So let's imagine, for example, that an emetophobe has managed to be persuaded to go to a doctor's surgery. How will she behave?

First, she will make sure she gets the first appointment of the day. This cuts down on waiting time and ensures she has the least exposure risk possible. I am assuming she is not waiting outside in a car but actually sitting in the waiting room. Her heart rate will be elevated from nervousness. Her stomach will be churning with nerves which will be doing no good to her intense feelings of panic and wanting to escape. She will have identified an escape route and also have knowledge of where the toilets are.

She will not touch the arms of the chairs, nor will she pick up a magazine to read in case it is infected (even though she probably knows that a germ or virus could not live on such a surface for long). She will sit away from everyone else and if possible next to an open window with her head turned towards it to breathe the 'clean' air. The most nerve-wracking thing of all for an emet will be noting who is also in the waiting room with them. People's faces will be judged on pallor. Are they pale and ashen? Do they look nauseous? Are they chatting and laughing happily with someone? If someone coughs, is it the type of cough that sounds like a chest infection or cold? Is there anyone sitting wrapped in a towel holding a bowl? If there is you can bet your life an emetophobe will not stay. She will leave, forgetting her own appointment and risking whatever wrath comes from her partner at home. She will then spend the next few days hardly eating and worrying about having caught that person's stomach virus.

Hospitals

Now, let's imagine that an emetophobe has to visit someone in hospital. First of all, he will have done everything possible to get out of visiting in the first place. If it's a distant relative or friend, he'll be able to come up with some excuse for not going, but if it is a close family member and he definitely has to go an emetophobe will start panicking days before.

On the appointed day, he might not eat at all, worrying and stressing about what he might see. At the hospital he will try to avoid looking at other people there, but if he spots anyone with a cardboard bowl near him then his anxiety levels will go through the roof. An emetophobe will be unable to stop himself checking on that person with the bowl. He will sneak glances, he will jump at every cough, he will ask the person they are there to see what is wrong with everyone else so that he can assess the vomiting risk. During all of this, the tension in an emetophobe's body will be rising. His pulse will race, he will be feeling sick and panicky himself. He may seem fidgety. He will definitely be anxious to leave. He may even have timed the visit for the last few minutes of visiting hours so that he has to leave soon, perhaps protesting to the patient that he would really have liked to stay for longer.

My husband's great aunt, a lady in her nineties, was admitted to hospital and I alternated days when I would visit her and my husband would go on the days that I missed. I never stayed long. I would just appear with the morning paper, ask her if she needed anything from home and then disappear. I did this four times until she caught a stomach bug going round the hospital. Thankfully, it was my husband's turn to visit that day. He came back from the hospital to tell me that his aunt had been ill whilst he'd been there and he'd even held the bowl for her.

I would like to be able to say that I wished her well and hoped she'd be better the next day, but that's not what I thought. All I could think of was not to let my husband come near me because he'd been touching a sick bowl whilst someone had vomited into it. I feared that he might be infected with a bug and therefore he might infect me. I hardly ate at all that night. I felt awful and miserable. Bugs seemed to be everywhere. I was convinced I was coming down with something and didn't get any sleep. I stayed awake most of the night, watching the stars and frantically working my way through a puzzle book to keep my mind off how my stomach was feeling. The next day I was exhausted and felt ill. I barely managed anything to eat at all. I refused to visit my husband's great aunt. I just couldn't go, even when he reported back that she was better and could come home. My husband never got sick from the hospital bug and neither did I, but the thought that I might was all it took.

The power of an emetophobe's thoughts, especially during a panic, wipes out all reason and logic. It's incredibly hard to explain, especially when the sufferer knows that the whole phobia is illogical and not rational at all. Emetophobes know they won't die from vomiting. They know that it only lasts for a few seconds. They know that other people do it and survive without any nasty after-effects, but that doesn't stop them panicking, or worrying, or getting anxious.

Seeking help

Many emetophobes will tell you (as they have told me and also reported on the emetophobic website forums) that when they have finally broached telling doctors, counsellors or therapists about their emetophobia (and are actually seeking help), the responses they have received have been varied and unfortunately, in the main, unhelpful. In the survey reported in Gut Reaction, 66 per cent of respondents had contacted their GPs about their emetophobia and of this percentage:

- 31 per cent found their GP to be understanding about their anxiety
- 23 per cent were referred to a clinical psychologist
- 23 per cent were referred to a psychiatrist
- 10 per cent saw a psychiatric nurse
- 5 per cent were referred to a counsellor
- 7 per cent were hospitalised to be fed via an intravenous (IV) drip
- 36 per cent were prescribed anti-emetic drugs
- 25 per cent were prescribed antidepressants
- 10 per cent were given diazepam
- 8 per cent were given tranquillizers
- 3 per cent were given propranolol
- 15 per cent were diagnosed as having irritable bowel syndrome (IBS)
- 6 per cent were diagnosed with migraines

- 6 per cent were diagnosed with balance problems or vertigo
- 7 per cent were diagnosed as having a duodenal/gastric ulcer.[1]

But the most astonishing facts that came from this survey were that a massive 92 per cent of respondents refuse medical treatment because of the side effects of the medicines and 97 per cent said that they were hesitant to take medication.

As you can see, there is a broad variety of reactions. A lot of GPs had to be told by the patient what emetophobia actually was and then dismissed it as an anxiety disorder and prescribed tranquillisers. So imagine yourself, you're feeling awful, you don't know why, but you're nauseous and have flu-like symptoms. You go to the doctor and you're prescribed a five-day course of antibiotics. No problem. But to emetophobes the visit to the surgery will cause problems mentally and emotionally. They will fear developing a further physical illness from having contracted something whilst sitting in the waiting room. If they're given medication the likelihood is (as shown in the survey results above) that only 8 per cent would actually take the medicine. Ninety-two per cent of emetophobes will read what it says on the medicine's information sheet and refuse to take it on the grounds that 'possible' side effects are nausea and vomiting. Even if this means an infection getting worse or pain getting unbearable, an emetophobe will refuse to take the medication.

It would be a wise precaution for those around emetophobes to know that they may pretend to be taking their tablets. They may disappear into the kitchen saying, 'I'll just take my tablet,' and make all the appropriate noises, getting a glass out of a cupboard, running a tap, rattling the packet or popping open a bottle. The tablet will be discreetly slipped into the bin or

---

1 Source: Dean, L. (1998) *Survey of Emetophobia Sufferers.* Gut Reaction. Available at www.gutreaction.freeuk.co.uk/survey-results.htm. Reprinted with permission.

hidden on their person for later disposal. If, as a non-emet, you become aware that this is the case, perhaps a telephone consultation with the doctor may be in order so that you can discuss the problem and ask if there is another medication the emetophobe can take that doesn't have any nauseating side effects (though having said that there aren't many drugs that fit that description).

No matter what you say, no matter how much you may argue with emetophobes that the medication will help them, they will refuse to take it. There will be nothing that can persuade them because the fear of actually suffering nausea and vomiting from a 'self-inflicted' course of medication would be anathema to them.

I was 17 weeks pregnant and my Hb iron levels were down to 7 when the normal range is 11–13. I was told that I needed to be in hospital immediately for a blood transfusion and can remember feeling calm, knowing that because I was pregnant they'd probably do this in Maternity where people weren't sick. So I willingly went into hospital.

I arrived in Maternity and they told me that because I was less than 18 weeks pregnant I had to go to casualty and get admitted through there. I was on my own and terrified. Casualty? All those people! It would be so busy, I'd have to wait ages and someone might be sick in the waiting area. I went to reception and gave them the name of the midwife who'd told me I needed a blood transfusion. I thought they'd send me straight through, but I was wrong. For an hour I watched a procession of people come through the doors with various injuries or illnesses. The worst were the children passing through to paediatric A&E. You could tell which ones looked sick. They had pale faces and clutched their stomachs. Gastro-enteritis, I assumed, holding my breath.

Eventually, I was called through and examined. Yes, I needed a blood transfusion, about three pints. I'd need to be admitted overnight as the process would take some time. I asked for a single room but they didn't have one available and put me in a ward with five others. It was mixed. Male. Female. Young and old. Two of them had cardboard sick bowls, one actually on the bed in front of the patient. I panicked and started shaking, trying my hardest not to cry in front of all these strangers who were looking at me kindly, the older generation wanting to ask me about the pregnancy.

When my husband arrived, I was in a right state. I asked him to pull the curtains around me for privacy and then I burst into tears. I was receiving blood through a tube in my arm and unaware that I was allowed to move around, so I felt trapped. I really felt nauseous, convinced that I was going to be sick. Beyond the curtain, I could hear someone coughing and choking and I was trying to figure out if it had been in the direction of the people with the bowls. I told my husband that I couldn't stay on a ward. I'd go crazy. It was too much. I needed to be alone, without sick people around me. He kindly went and had a quick word with the nurse in charge.

A side room had become available and they agreed to put me in there. I was so thankful I cried even more. I walked out of the ward attached to my pole without looking at anyone, but being incredibly aware of the 'bowl beds'. In the side room I relaxed somewhat. It was late at night and I was still being given my first pint of blood. The nurse brought me some pre-packaged sandwiches, tuna fish. I was hungry, but because of my nerves I couldn't eat anything. My husband left, promising to return the next morning to bring me home.

By one in the morning, I'd been given all the blood and I was 'unhooked' from the tube. I was desperate to sleep. The panic attacks had exhausted me and I felt so weary, but all I could hear was coughing and retching from the room next to me. Telephones kept ringing and I could hear the night shift talking. My stomach churned like mad and I began to get stomach cramps. They were really bad and I went to the toilet and suffered some diarrhoea. It was awful. I associate diarrhoea with stomach bugs and sickness and soon enough another panic attack was assailing me. I had to keep going to the toilet for the next two hours and by three in the morning I was starting to get really bad. I just wanted to be home. I went out to the nurses and told them how bad I felt and asked whether I could discharge myself, that I'd feel better if I could just be at home.

They told me I could discharge myself but it wasn't advisable for the sake of the baby and my own health. They needed to test my Hb levels in the morning and see if I needed more blood. I couldn't believe it. I just wanted to get out of there, but I knew I had to put the baby inside of me first so I asked if I could have an anti-emetic. The answer was no. They wouldn't give them to me because I was pregnant. The next four hours to seven o'clock were the longest in my life. When no one turned up to take my blood at the allotted hour I went in search of the phlebotomist myself. I was the happiest woman alive when they said I could go home.

I think it's quite plain that doctors in particular need to understand just how being in a surgery and visiting a doctor makes an emetophobe feel. It has been suggested that if a doctor knows a patient is emetophobic then they should allow that patient to have more telephone consultations or home visits. This may help at the beginning when emetophobes need assistance to explain how they feel and why. But what should happen in the long run? Emetophobes shouldn't restrict their lives and hide away. If they do, they run a strong risk of letting the phobia control their lives.

In the main, emetophobes fear stomach viruses most. They are the ultimate fear for this type of phobic. Unfortunately, over the last few years, it has become noticeable that the UK in particular seems to suffer a Norovirus epidemic during the winter, mostly around Christmas. School numbers are depleted by sick children. Adults stay away from work. Hospital wards have been closed down because of the virus.

When the winter vomiting virus takes hold, it really does strike fear into an emetophobe. It seems so prevalent, so contagious. Many find themselves questioning whether it is contactable by touch only or whether it is airborne. Some are so frightened that they will not leave their houses during an outbreak in order to prevent infection. They do all of their shopping online and go to great lengths to avoid people.

During a woman's menstrual cycle it can be quite natural to feel a little off-colour before a period starts. For some female emetophobes this can be a time of great worry. They know that every four weeks or so they will feel nauseated and ill. So some female emets do not worry about serious weight loss from not being able to eat because they know that when their periods stop due to undereating they can also prevent the regular monthly nausea they experience. Even though logically they also know that this may have an effect on their future fertility and chances of conceiving a baby, the fear of the nausea is greater. The fear of what might happen is the driving force. They 'might' get infected; they 'might' get sick; they 'might' vomit. Because of this fear they shut themselves away from the world.

Dentists

Dental surgeries can also be a huge problem for emetophobes. Many will not visit a dentist for a variety of reasons: the lying flat, all those instruments in the mouth, the inability to swallow, the fear of choking on saliva, the need for treatment that results in bleeding and blood entering the stomach and making them feel sick.

Consequently, many emetophobes have problems with their teeth, especially those who suck mints constantly as a way of dealing with constant nausea. The high sugar content in their mouths adds to the complications of decay and before long they begin to experience pains and toothaches that need dealing with. They may experience a lot of pain while 'waiting for it to pass' until eventually they realise that the problem is permanent and needs to be sorted. This may result in emets going to the doctor for anti-anxiety medication or trying to deal with it on their own, but whichever way they choose going to a dentist is not a good experience.

CHAPTER EIGHT

Holidays

I've already mentioned how one of my holidays went when I was a little girl. What I didn't mention was that from that year onwards every time we went back I expected the same thing to happen to me. This usually meant I'd spend the entire time anxiously fretting whilst pretending to everyone else that I was having a great time. It didn't do my nerves any good! But at least my childhood holidays were only in Ingoldmells. My mother has never flown and never wanted to and my father is quite happy with trips to the east coast of England. It is only now that I wonder how I might have coped if my parents had told me we were going to Spain or some other country that required a plane to get you there.

As a child you don't get much say in where you go for holidays, but as an adult you tend to be the one who gets to choose. Generally most emets, almost 90 per cent of respondents, stated that they had difficulty in travelling and 94 per cent reported that they were unable to go away on holidays.[1] Take a moment and imagine never having a holiday. Unfortunately, this is how it is for most emetophobes. Home is their safe environment and many of them have difficulty just going into town to

---

1 Dean, L. (1998) *Survey of Emetophobia Sufferers.* Gut Reaction. Available at www.gut-reaction.freeserve.co.uk/survey-results.htm. Reprinted with permission.

do some shopping, never mind getting into a car or on to a train, plane or boat.

Flying

Personally, I was adamant that I'd never get on a plane. My husband has been to almost every country there is and he could not understand my reticence. He knew about my phobia. He listened to me explain that I had absolutely no fear of crashing or anything like that, I just knew I wouldn't be able to handle getting airsick or seeing someone else get airsick. Somehow though he persuaded me to give it a try. Our first child was 18 months old, our twins were four months old. His reasoning went along the lines that he wanted our children to travel as much as he had. Was I going to hold them back just because of a little phobia? Motherly guilt is an excellent weapon, isn't it?

So I got on a flight to the United States. It was 18 January and we were booked for a fortnight's holiday in Clearwater, Florida. I wanted to see Busch Gardens and determinedly grabbed the bull by its horns. I had my anti-emetics and took one before I got on the flight. My husband held my hand and told me take-off and landing were the worst parts and he felt sure I'd enjoy it, which I did, until four hours into the flight. I noticed the guy across the aisle from me had placed his air-sickness bag on the seat next to him. Inside, I just flipped. Anxiety and panic hit me like a hurricane and my stomach churned. Then the pilot announced that we were turning around and heading out of US airspace because someone had written a bomb threat in the toilet.

We diverted to Iceland. My knuckles were white as I gripped the seat, trying to keep control of the nausea and fright while the trip fast became my worst nightmare. It was four months since 9/11 and there we were on a threatened flight. I'd been watching Sky News when the planes hit the World Trade Centre. I can remember watching it in total shock and now here I was with my husband and young son (my twins were with their grandparents), still a baby almost, on a terrifying flight. We made it to Iceland. It was freezing and we were dressed for spring. There were men with machine guns. We were questioned by police and had our handwriting tested. All the time I wanted to be somewhere on my own but we were not allowed to leave the airport. We spent our time milling about in the airport lounge until three in the morning when they sent us to a hotel.

I was exhausted. My nerves had been constantly on a tight leash since 6 o'clock that morning and here I was, 21 hours later, finally being allowed to hide from the world and relax, facing the knowledge that I needed to get on another plane to get back home, another two-hour flight. I could do that, right? Apparently not. Despite taking my anti-emetics and pretending I was the big brave mummy my son needed me to be, I took one look at the broccoli and kedgeree breakfast served on the plane and knew that if I didn't get off the flight I was going to be sick and I was going to be sick really bad!

It was a full-blown panic attack. The stewards moved me to the back of the plane where there were three empty seats. I felt slightly calmer knowing that the toilets were right there next to me, but I couldn't get out of my panic. The nausea was getting worse. I was convinced I was going to be sick and imagined how it might be. I tried to picture myself afterwards but couldn't see it except for me being a gibbering wreck. It suddenly hit me that I needed fresh air. If it hadn't been for my son and husband being on the same flight as me I would have gone up to the doors and opened them. It may sound ridiculous but I really thought it would help rid me of the sensation of being trapped on the plane. That is how strongly emetophobia can grip you.

I can look back at it now in wonder, amazed I would have those sorts of thoughts just to ease my nausea, but right then the sickness was the worse thing to me. Nothing else mattered. I was so relieved to get my feet on solid ground at London Heathrow airport. This is a dramatic story and not one that every emet will experience as most of them would not get even as far as an airport. They might go to look at planes taking off and landing with their children or husband, but they certainly wouldn't get on one.

Other forms of transport

Many emetophobes have reported feeling just as bad when they have tried to brave other forms of transport.[2] Boats and ships seem to be big no-go areas. When asked why, they reported that the idea of possibly getting seasick themselves was just as bad as fearing that others might also get seasick. They wouldn't feel relaxed wandering around a cruise liner in case one of the people standing at the railings looking out to sea might not just be enjoying the view but about to be sick. Another fear about being on a boat was that if they got on one and it was as bad as they feared, there was no way they'd be able to get off quickly. They could hardly arrange emergency helicopter evacuation. Even the knowledge that there is an on-board doctor or medical crew on most large liners and cruise ships did nothing to alleviate fears.

A lot of emetophobes have to catch trains to get themselves to work. This also proved to be a source of large amounts of stress and anxiety. One emet reported deliberately walking along the train to find the emptiest compartment (not easy when she was travelling during rush hour) just so she could sit on her own and not face the possibility of someone getting travel sick. Another took his laptop with him or a book, just so that he could keep his head down and not see anyone else for the same reason. He didn't even need a laptop for his job and would tell his colleagues at work that he used it to play games on his long journey into work.

---

2 Dean, L. (1998) *Survey of Emetophobia Sufferers.* Gut Reaction. Available at www.gut-reaction.freeserve.co.uk/survey-results.htm. Reprinted with permission.

Buses scored high on the anxiety scale due to the smell, lack of cleanliness in general and dizzying patterns on the seats, along with the need to check fellow passengers for paleness or possible illness. Most emetophobes who use buses report sitting in the seats directly behind the driver so that they are slightly separated from other passengers and can also see the road ahead. They also feel somewhat reassured by being close to the exit and comforted by the fact that if they did need to get off the bus quickly, they could press a bell and leave at any stop.

Cars are the most popular form of transport. Most emetophobes prefer to be the driver rather than a passenger. This has nothing to do with the issue of being in control of the vehicle. Being the driver allows emetophobes to focus on what they have to do to drive the car safely, concentrating on roadsigns and directions. Basically, it keeps their minds off their stomachs. The other benefit that a car provides above other forms of transport is being able to be alone without worrying about anyone else inside the vehicle.

For outings with friends or work colleagues, most emetophobes will offer to meet the group at a designated meeting point rather than travel in a minibus with the others. They will always come up with a plausible reason for doing so if their colleagues do not know about the emetophobia. The idea of travelling with a group of friends to a party is horrific because of the concern and worry about whether those friends would already have started drinking, who might get sick on the bus, etc.

Only a small minority feel they cannot travel in any type of vehicle. As a result these emetophobes confine themselves mostly to home and only make it out to local shops they can walk to. One respondent said that she would like to be able to drive but did not feel that she'd be able to get through any driving lessons as these would take her away from her 'safe zone' (which she defined as being the few streets near her home) and trap her in a car for at least an hour.

Many emets reported that they tended to stay at home whilst their partners went on exotic holidays. For some, this issue also raised problems as the phobic sufferers found themselves wondering about the fidelity of their partners as most believed that living with and looking after an emet was difficult. Clearly suffering from emetophobia is not simple, but has wide-reaching implications for everyone involved – not just the sufferer (I explore the effects of living with an emetophobe in Chapter 17).

CHAPTER NINE

Food Worries

Food in itself can be an enormous psychological threat and worry to an emetophobe. The majority of emetophobes are underweight and actually sometimes confused with being anorexic. Indeed there are many reports of sufferers seeing their doctor and being referred to counsellors to help them with their 'eating disorder' of anorexia nervosa or bulimia. (No emetophobe would ever want to make him- or herself sick by sticking fingers down his or her throat, but the theory that they are some sort of 'closet bulimic' appears to be quite popular, despite being totally untrue.)

It is easy to see how sufferers of emetophobia might be labelled anorexic. Anorexics control their food consumption with extreme rules. Emetophobes also control what goes into their mouths as food. The connection here with the emetophobia is quite clear.

Sickness and vomiting involves food or liquids being ejected from the stomach through the force of muscles that control the opening. Food and liquids are stored in the stomach and we need food and liquids to survive. Some foods may be contaminated, some might not be cooked properly, so emetophobes will be extremely careful about just what goes into the stomach to protect themselves as much as possible from an internal attack caused by their own mistakes.

Let's look at this in more detail. Food intake is very important as we all know. We all need food to survive and it is generally accepted that we need a certain number of calories in our food intake for our bodies to perform at an optimum level. The suggested daily calorific intake for women is 2000 and for men 2500 calories. This daily calorie intake should be made up from all the food groups, including the recommended five fruit/vegetable portions per day, proteins, carbohydrates, minerals, vitamins, etc. that the body requires to work well.

Now it is imperative to understand that an emetophobe knows this information too. Remember that phobics are quite knowledgeable about germs, infection and bacteria and they also know about food, hygiene, cooking and diet. They know what is healthy and what they need to eat to have a healthy body without deficiencies, but they also know the possible dangers of eating certain foods (such as chicken or fish that hasn't been stored or cooked properly).

Safe foods

Many emetophobes will have a mental list of 'safe foods'. Generally, this means any sort of dried or packaged food that has no possible way of causing food poisoning or sickness. Some of these 'safe foods' are listed below:

- bananas
- nuts
- crisps
- biscuits
- cakes
- oranges
- tinned spaghetti/beans
- chips
- pasta
- chocolate
- crackers.

This list only includes a few foods that are actually healthy. Fruit contained within a protective skin is considered safe because the flesh has not been exposed to any germs or bacteria. Other fruit such as apples and pears are not considered safe because they have to be washed before consumption. There is always the fear that not all of the germs have been washed off. Because of this, many emetophobes will avoid these kinds of fruits, or will peel off the skin and eat only the internal flesh.

The rest of the list contains what most doctors and dieticians would consider unhealthy foods, high in sugar and fat, and they are right. These foods aren't healthy for the body if eaten in large quantities. But to emetophobes they're safe, and that is what matters more than anything, especially if they are hungry and need to eat something quickly.

Having looked at the list, you might wonder why emetophobes aren't all dangerously obese. Eating so much fat and foods high in sugar and calorie content surely must mean that they should all be overweight? However, this is not the case. Another great worry to an emetophobe would be overeating. A symptom of overeating is feeling nauseous and sick and, as I'm sure you're aware from having read this far, an emetophobe will not risk feeling like that for anything in the world. Plus, some of the foods on the list, such as chocolate and cake, are extremely sweet. Eating large amounts would result in someone feeling very sick indeed. So even though all of these foods are considered 'safe', they are still eaten in small quantities. Therefore emetophobes do not generally consume as many calories as they need per day to ensure that their bodies are in their optimal condition. And they do know this.

Emetophobes do not have body dysmorphia. They do not look in the mirror and see a fat body when in reality it is thin. They see their thin bodies. They see the thin arms and legs, their skinny ribs and their hipbones sticking out. More than anything they'd love to be a normal weight, but to achieve that they would have to eat a wider range of food in much greater quantities.

To an emetophobe this just seems an impossible task. In fact one doctor who saw me as a young child told me that because I'd spent so long eating small quantities at mealtimes, my stomach had in fact shrunk and was incapable of eating larger normal portions that other people were able to eat. Is this true? Absolutely, but even so I also know that if I trained myself over time to eat steadily increasing amounts, I'd be able to eat larger portions with more calories and be taking in the proper diet an adult female requires. I would, in effect, be growing my stomach, but I find this hard to do. It is almost impossible even now. Every time I try, I feel as if I have overeaten which makes me feel so uncomfortable and sick that I can't eat for hours. When I do, I can only eat a small amount and then I feel I'm right back at square one. I can see that if I want to be a normal weight for my height then I have to eat more, but I can't put myself through the suffering of feeling sick after every meal because I feel as if I've overeaten. I'm back where I started, eating little and often because that doesn't make me ill.

Danger foods

So if there is a list of 'safe foods', what about 'danger foods'? High on most emetophobes' 'dangerous food' list are chicken and fish. We all know that if these foods aren't cooked properly there is extreme likelihood of food poisoning. Beef and lamb can be served pink but chicken cannot. Fish needs to be cooked thoroughly and most of it eaten whilst hot; if not you're in danger of getting sick.

An emetophobe is very cautious around chicken in particular. Some emetophobes will even refuse to have it in the house for fear of contaminating other food items in the fridge. They will don gloves to handle a raw chicken and rinse it thoroughly under the tap. They then rinse out and bleach their sink if they've just cleaned a chicken in it. It will be overcooked rather than done to perfection, just to make sure it has been cooked properly. Even though this means that the meat is inevitably dry, emetophobes prefer it this way because then they know they're safe.

Despite all these precautions, emetophobes will still examine the chicken when they dissect it for the slightest trace of pink in the meat. If seen, the chicken will be discarded for no one to eat and the meal will end up being vegetarian. When the chicken has been served up, emetophobes will examine their piece a second time for pinkness. After eating chicken emetophobes will usually spend some time in a state of anxiety, wondering if they took every precaution and whether they'll still get ill from food poisoning. Every twinge in the abdomen, every strange sensation or rumble of the stomach, will be associated with eating chicken. Emetophobes will only breathe a sigh of relief when they start to feel hungry for their next meal. And that's just for chicken!

Fish tends to be eaten in small portions too. Larger portions go cool because it takes so long to eat them and an emetophobe will not eat cold fish. Again, the fish will be overcooked and falling to pieces before an emetophobe will eat it. Vegetables are always washed and peeled if necessary and again overcooked just to make sure.

Combined foods are a big worry. This can mean anything from shepherd's pie to meat pie to lasagne or chicken wrapped in bacon – in general, any sort of food combined with another in a large parcel to make another dish. For example, some dishes require a cut of meat to be stuffed with herbs, or garlic butter, or even another meat. An emetophobe will worry that because the meat has been stuffed with something else the dish is so much larger and will take longer to cook properly all the way through, especially if it has a pastry crust. Many emetophobes will only eat dishes such as these if they can cut them open through the middle and test the centre for heat. If it's piping hot then they might consider eating the side pieces (because the suspicion of it being undercooked will still be there) and they'll test each piece to make sure it is perfectly hot and thoroughly cooked. The drier, the better!

Another set of foods that rates highly on an emetophobe's 'danger list' are takeaways. Fish and chips tend to be trusted as they always seem to be piping hot. Emets can even stand there and time how long the fish has been cooked for. But when it comes to pizzas, or Chinese and Indian takeaways, then I'm afraid to say that even though emets would love to be able to try out these foods, they will tend to refuse to eat them. This is because emets have not seen the state of cleanliness in the takeaway kitchen. They have no idea whether the cooks have taken all the precautions emets would take in their own kitchen and they also have no idea where most of the meat has come from. If emets do decide to eat a takeaway, they tend to order the foods that are considered 'safer' such as plain boiled rice, cooked pineapple, or onion bhajis; foods that on their own have much lower risks of causing food poisoning (in an emet's mind).

Drinks

Now, let's move on to drinks. How harmful or threatening can a simple drink be? To an emet, alcoholic drinks pose tremendous risk. People who get drunk can throw up either right there during the drinking session or else during the hangover suffered the morning after. An emetophobe will never get drunk because of this. Emetophobes are generally teetotallers, or if they do imbibe a little it will only be one glass – two at a push. They will simply not take the risk of suffering drunkenness or a hangover. They do not see the point of imposing the suffering on themselves via a self-inflicted route. Because of this you will also discover that emetophobes will greatly fear their partner/spouse drinking and getting drunk. If a partner wishes to have a drink on a night out or gets a few cans or bottles in for the home, the emetophobe will try to impose restrictions on the drinking:

- 'Please don't get drunk.'
- 'You'll only have the one, won't you?'
- 'Make that bottle last for a few days.'
- 'If you get drunk then you'll have to sleep elsewhere.'

This last condition can be somewhat of a problem. Many partners of emetophobes don't see why their partner is so scared of them getting drunk, especially if the emetophobe has not confided in his or her partner/spouse about the phobia. The partners/spouses want to have a drink. They want to let their hair down occasionally, relax and enjoy themselves. This is not very easy to do when you've got someone worrying about every sip that passes your lips.

One emetophobe confessed to making her husband sleep in the car in their driveway after a night at a wedding party. Her partner was so drunk he could hardly stand. When they got home (she came back separately in a different taxi in case he was sick during the journey), she let him into the car with a couple of carrier bags to be sick into and locked him in all night, letting him out in the morning after she'd sent her daughter out to the car to check that he hadn't been sick and was safe to let back in.

Other phobics have confessed sending their partners away to stay at their parents' house if they threaten to drink near them. One emetophobe reported that on her honeymoon her new husband got so drunk that she asked the hotel to give him another room and they didn't sleep together for three whole nights. Even then she spent the night with tissues jammed into her ears to stop hearing retching noises when the kind-hearted hotel staff put the husband in the room next door.

Socialising

All of these problems with food and alcohol make it very difficult for an emetophobe who gets invited out to eat, whether just as a couple or as part of a group, a dinner party, or work do.

Imagine having all these fears about food. Imagine for a moment that you're sitting at a table for an important dinner, surrounded by people you don't know very well, and a plate of food is put in front of you. For non-phobics, this wouldn't be a problem. They'd eat the food, make polite conversation and try to enjoy themselves, being sociable. But for emetophobes, they'd be sitting there worrying about how they were going to eat such a large amount and whether it was prepared in sanitary conditions. Was the salad washed thoroughly? Was the meat rinsed under the tap before cooking? Was it cooked properly? What has it been stuffed with? How can I eat all that food without it making me ill? How can I leave most of it on my plate without insulting my host and having everyone ask me if it was all right?

For a lot of reasons, many emetophobes won't actually accept dinner dates. They won't go to group socials, working lunches, friends' houses, pubs or restaurants for a meal. They'd like to, would love to do it even, but the stress and worry is usually too much.

I remember a wedding I was invited to and afterwards there was a sit-down meal in a very posh hall. I'd made it through the wedding service and was wondering what would be on the menu. It was an emetophobe's worst nightmare – chicken. A starter of a mushroom melody was served in a box of filo pastry. At the time, I hated mushrooms. I couldn't stand the way they felt in my mouth, all slimy and musty. I nibbled at the pastry box and pushed the mushrooms onto my husband's plate. People around me (whom I didn't know) gave me some funny looks. I can remember smiling nervously, knowing that they were already looking at me and assuming that they now knew why I was so thin. I assumed that most of them thought I was anorexic.

Then came the chicken, served with potatoes and green beans, tied together in bacon. It looked okay. It appeared to be properly cooked. I started eating but as soon as I got deeper into the chicken, I saw that it was pink – bright pink. My stomach recoiled and I started to panic. Oh goodness, I'd eaten pink chicken. There was still the rest of the reception to go and the evening do, and then there was a two-hour drive to get back home.

The panic attack began. My legs began to shake, my hands trembled. I didn't want to eat any more. My husband was talking to someone else and couldn't see me and I was watching all these people around me tucking into their chicken, which even I could see was pink on every single plate! I was amazed! Didn't these people know? Finally, my husband turned back to me and asked me what the matter was. I told him. It was the chicken. It was pink, not cooked properly. My husband frowned. What could we do? Stand up and tell everyone that they were all tucking into something that would poison them? Upset the bride and groom on their big day?

He told me to not eat any more and we both put our forks and knives together to indicate we were finished and watched everyone else enjoy their food. My nerves were in shreds. I honestly do not know how I sat there, waiting for the stomach pains to begin. I noted the positions of the toilets and tried to work out just how I'd be able to dash to one if the need arose. Yet the hall was so full of guests. What if they all started getting sick? How would I cope? I desperately wanted to go home and pleaded with my husband to come up with some excuse so we could go. The waiters came around to collect the plates.

'Did you not enjoy your meal, sir?' they asked my husband.

'The chicken was pink,' he whispered, trying to be diplomatic.

The waiter simply smiled and answered, 'That's because it was stuffed with cranberries, sir.'

You cannot imagine the relief. I wasn't embarrassed at all. It was simply relief. I'd hardly eaten a thing so when the pudding was served I ate it, relishing the fact that I could trust it. You'd think that would be the end of the worry for me then, but it wasn't. During the speeches it suddenly occurred to me that if the chicken had been stuffed with cranberries and was coloured pink, then we wouldn't really have known if it was cooked properly, would we? An undercooked chicken would not have been noticed because of the staining from the cranberry juice.

The panic set in again and I spent the rest of that miserable day waiting to get stomach pains and/or be sick. I pressured my husband every chance I got to take us home. I just wanted to leave. Everyone else was happy and enjoying the special day, but all I could think about was eating the chicken. I didn't relax about it until three days later when I figured that if I were going to get food poisoning it would have happened by then. Too much? Paranoid? You bet it was, but when you're in the middle of an emetophobic panic then logic simply flies out of the window.

Shopping

Food problems aren't just about safe foods and danger foods or making sure that things have been cooked properly. For an emetophobe, there's worry everywhere when it comes to all types of food. For example, the fresh fruit and vegetables displayed loose in supermarkets all look lovely and are good to eat. They are healthy for you. But emetophobes may worry about the people who have been rummaging through them and touching them. How can they know the state of health of the previous shopper, or the previous ten shoppers? They can't. Emetophobes will be moving the trays and selecting their fruit and vegetables from a couple of layers down where they hope no one else has been. When they get the fresh produce home it will still be thoroughly cleaned and washed just in case.

When browsing the supermarket shelves for food, emetophobes will pick the item with the longest sell-by date on it, assuming that to be the freshest. Having said that, if it's a delicatessan item such as slices of cold meat, once the packet has been opened at home they will only use it on that day. Even if they're left with many beautiful slices of meat and the sell-by or best-before date is over two weeks away, they will still dispose of the meat just to be safe.

Ready-prepared meals can be questionable for emetophobes. They have no idea how that food was mixed. Generally, when served, these meals do not look particularly appetising to them and they will only eat the parts around the edges where they assume it is properly cooked. Therefore ready-meals are something used sparingly and when in a rush.

Frozen foods are considered safe. All, without question, are in packaging, so it doesn't matter who's been rummaging through them. The food inside has not been touched by other people's hands.

Another big no-no for an emetophobe are the 'taste and try' displays you see in some of the larger shops. A new product is out on the market and they offer samples of it for you to taste. It's usually neatly cut up and sliced and waiting for you to take a bite. Emetophobes will not do this. They have no idea how long the food has been sitting in that shop with masses of people walking by. People who may have illnesses or be recovering from illnesses might have touched the food, so it will usually be politely refused.

What about complimentary food, the type that sits on a bar or reception desk that you can help yourself to? It can be nuts, sweets, fruit or savouries. An emetophobe will definitely not touch any of these items. Even the average Joe Public has heard of tests done on these offerings and the amount of faecal matter found on them being disgusting. Why would an emetophobe risk eating that?

Food, in all its forms, causes great concern to phobics. They need it to live and they'd love to feel that they could eat as much as they need to stay healthy, but they just can't. The thoughts get in the way, those pervading thoughts that have been with them so long, telling them to be careful, to double-check, not to eat too much in case they overload their stomach and make themselves feel sick.

Most emets try to ignore the thoughts. They get on with eating, forcing themselves to have chicken and fish because the rest of the family is eating it and knowing they can't live on sandwiches. But even as they're doing it, they know they will spend the rest of the evening after the meal waiting to feel ill, worrying and fretting until the next day and the next. Some days it's easy; others it's not. But they use coping strategies to get themselves through it, knowing that if they don't they'll probably end up in hospital being force-fed, and none of them wants that.

CHAPTER TEN

Medication

Practically all emetophobes I spoke to during the course of writing and researching this book admitted to using or owning some form of medication that they trusted to help them get through the tough times when they felt sick, or felt that a panic attack was going to start. In general, it appeared that a few tried and trusted drug names kept coming up, so I thought I'd go over each of these and explain why to an emetophobe they work and the psychological effect they also seem to have. This list encompasses anti-emetics, which I will deal with first as they are considered the most important by emetophobes, and then various others such as tranquillisers. None of these medications is being recommended and readers should always consult their doctor before using them.

Motilium

Available in tablet or suspension form, it is sold as Motilium 10 (domperidone). This drug is to be used by adults only and is a non-prescriptive drug. Motilium is used to treat nausea and vomiting. Its active ingredient is domperidone which is an anti-emetic that is also useful in ridding a sufferer of feelings of abdominal bloating, fullness and stomach discomfort.

How does it work and why? Domperidone acts by blocking the dopamine receptors in the brain, an area called the chemoreceptor trigger zone (CTZ). The CTZ is activated by nerve messages from the stomach when an irritant is present.

Once activated, the CTZ sends messages to the vomiting centre of the brain, which in turn sends messages to the gut, causing the vomiting reflex.

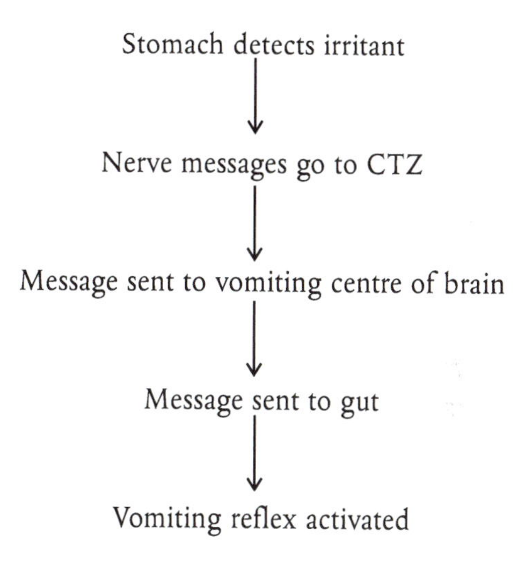

Therefore, Motilium acts by blocking the messages that arrive in the CTZ, preventing any further messages being sent to the vomiting centre, thereby reducing nausea. Motilium blocks the dopamine receptors and once the nausea is reduced the sensation that a sufferer might vomit is reduced and disappears.

Domperidone also blocks dopamine receptors found in the upper end of the digestive system. This results in a tightening of the muscles at the entry to the stomach, relaxation of the muscles at the exit of the stomach and increases contractions of the main stomach itself to encourage it to empty quickly. This action also helps physically prevent vomiting. The medication is not recommended for long-term use.

Motilium contains lactose and the suspension contains sorbitol so anyone allergic to either of these ingredients should not take this particular medication. The drug information states that you should use Motilium with caution if you have decreased liver function or with infants. Prolonged usage is said to severely decrease kidney function and it is not to be used if you have a stomach or intestinal perforation, bleeding from the gut, cancer of the pituitary, an obstruction of the gut, are pregnant or allergic to any of the ingredients. Side effects listed include diarrhoea, enlargement of male breasts, breast pain, twitching, high blood prolactin, stomach cramps, low libido and itchy rashes. Domperidone is also in Vivadone tablets (prescription only).

Maxolon High Dose

The active ingredient in Maxolon High Dose is metoclopramide hydrochloride, which should be used with caution if you are epileptic. It is not to be used if you are breastfeeding. The details for this medication and the way it works are the same as for Motilium 10. It is available only on prescription.

Stemetil

Stemetil is mainly used for psychosis and the prevention of nausea and vomiting. Its main ingredient is prochlorperazine, which belongs to a group of medications known as the phenothiazine antipsychotics. It is sometimes referred to as a major tranquilliser. It acts by blocking a variety of brain receptors, particularly the dopamine receptors. An excessive amount of dopamine in the brain results in overstimulation of these receptors, which can result in a psychotic illness. Prochlorperazine blocks this.

The drug is used with schizophrenics and those who wish to block the area of the brain that controls the vomiting centre. It can also be used to treat nausea and vomiting caused by inner ear disorders. Its further uses include anxiety, inner ear problems, mania, Ménière's syndrome, nausea and vomiting, psychotic illness and schizophrenia.

Do not take alcohol with this drug. Use it with caution if you have an abnormal heart rhythm, abnormal muscle weakness, closed angle glaucoma, are elderly, have an enlarged prostate gland, epilepsy, hypothyroidism, kidney disease, liver disease, low blood potassium, Parkinson's disease, or an adrenal tumour. It is not to be used during pregnancy. Stemetil is only available on prescription.

During the survey, 10 per cent of emetophobes declared that they had been prescribed diazepam by their doctors, along with a number of respondents reporting that they had been given antidepressants and/or tranquillisers.

Diazepam

Diazepam is a prescription only drug and its main use is to control convulsions and severe anxiety. It is a type of medicine called a benzodiazepine, used for its sedative and anxiety-relieving effects. It works by acting on the GABA receptors in the brain, where a neurotransmitter (GABA) is released. GABA acts in the body as a natural nerve-calming agent. It helps keep the nerve activity in the brain in balance and can also induce sleepiness, reduction of anxiety and muscle relaxation. Diazepam increases the GABA in the brain, therefore increasing the body's ability to be calm.

Diazepam has several uses. It calms severe anxiety and agitation and works particularly well in bipolar affective disorder. Oral diazepam is a good short-term treatment for anxiety and insomnia, night terrors and sleepwalking in children. It decreases the amount of time it takes a person to fall asleep, yet also increases the amount of time spent asleep. Drowsiness can persist into the next day.

However, the drug can only be used in the short term as there is a high likelihood that the body may become dependent on it. If you are prescribed this drug, your doctor should be consulted regarding how to decrease the medication and come off it slowly as there can be some harsh withdrawal symptoms if you stop completely.

Irritable bowel syndrome

In the survey by Gut Reaction, 15 per cent of emetophobic respondents were also diagnosed with irritable bowel syndrome (IBS) which gets worse with stress and can be a distressing condition. This 15 per cent had been given medication to help the condition such as Buscopan and Lomotil, but some felt that they couldn't take anything 'medical' because of the side effects of the drug. Some of these respondents continued to suffer in silence, putting up with their condition, whereas others researched the illness and took 'less worrying' measures by altering their diets and drinking peppermint tea, which seemed to help ease the painful cramps and wind.

Feeling sick

The emets in the survey were asked how often they felt sick or felt they were going to be sick each month and this is how they answered:

- 26 per cent experienced nausea six times a month
- 16 per cent experienced nausea 7 to 12 times a month
- 22 per cent experienced nausea 13 to 20 times a month
- 14 per cent experienced nausea every day.[1]

It has been suggested by Dr David Veale, a leading researcher on vomit phobia, that the reason emetophobes experience such high levels of nausea is because they are so sensitive to it because they fear it; that in reality if they didn't fear being sick then they

---

1 Dean, L. (1998) *Survey of Emetophobia Sufferers.* Gut Reaction. Available at www.gut-reaction.freeserve.co.uk/survey-results.htm. Reprinted with permission.

wouldn't actually notice the nausea.[2] Knowing this fact and living with it are two different things entirely. Of the numbers above, those that experienced nausea stated that when it began:

- 35 per cent felt sick for three hours
- 11 per cent felt sick for four to six hours
- 5 per cent felt sick for 7 to 11 hours
- 8 per cent felt sick for 12 to 24 hours
- 12 per cent felt sick for 24 to 72 hours.[3]

These are high figures and something doctors and others need to be aware of.

As soon as emetophobes detect the nausea, whether they know logically or not that the likelihood of their being sick is close to zero, just the fact that they feel sick or have felt sick is enough to set off a chain reaction that can last for up to three days or more. When sickness is experienced, they question everything they have done: what they have eaten; what they have touched; the last time they washed their hands; whom they have been in contact with who might have been ill, or looked dodgy. They will then stop eating, or at least ration what they eat, managing on soup or dry crackers, a small piece of toast or 'something safe'. This paranoia about being sick will last for days until the emetophobe feels that the danger has passed.

During these stressful and worrying times, emetophobes will take anti-emetics or anxiety medication if they have it. If they are taking anti-emetics two or three times a day for three days, a couple of times each week, then the effects of using this medication too often could cause some harm (as shown in the description of Motilium 10).

---

2 Veale, D. and Lambrou, C. (2007) *The Psychopathology of Vomit Phobia.* Gut Reaction. Available at www.gut-reaction.freeserve.co.uk/drdveale.htm. Reprinted with permission.

3 Dean, L. (1998) *Survey of Emetophobia Sufferers.* Gut Reaction. Available at www.gut-reaction.freeserve.co.uk/survey-results.htm. Reprinted with permission.

CHAPTER ELEVEN

Emetophobic Mothers

This is a difficult chapter, as I am a mother myself and also emetophobic. Thankfully, my phobia does not affect me as badly as some of the examples in this book, but there are some emetophobic mothers who are terrified of being with their own children. Imagine that for a moment, if you will. Imagine being terrified to hold your own children, to kiss them, cuddle them, comfort them after a bad day; not feel able to play with them or just enjoy their company. And why? Because their child may be harbouring a stomach virus that hasn't taken effect yet, or their child has been sick or had diarrhoea. The emetophobic mother just cannot be with her child because she's terrified of catching the virus herself.

Anyone reading this who is not emetophobic may think that this is a terribly selfish reaction and that surely it can't be that bad, that things are different with your own children and surely the fear can be overcome? Well, I'm afraid the answer is no. They cannot overcome that fear, even for their children. Yes, it is selfish and it makes emetophobic mothers feel awful about how they are reacting, guilty and shameful and cowardly, but they just cannot do it.

Usually, it has already taken a great deal of courage to become a mother in the first place. Many emetophobic women won't even contemplate pregnancy, despite yearning to be a mother. They live their lives childless because the phobia has more control over their thoughts than the desire for a child. However, there are some emetophobic women who feel brave enough to take on the nauseating challenges of pregnancy and birth, just so that their lives are not controlled in all ways by this terrible phobia.

> I would love to have another child. I've only got one and I'd love to give him a little brother or sister, but I just can't do it. I can't go through that again. (Jackie, 43)

Babies

When emetophobes have babies, most are pleasantly surprised to find that they can quite easily deal with a little bit of posseting and burped up milk from a baby. After all, they know it is only milk. All babies do it. They know it isn't because of a stomach bug. Therefore most emetophobic mothers would happily admit that they can deal with baby sick. This all changes, however, when the baby goes on to solid foods and the consistency, content and colour changes. This posseting looks more like sick and even though some emets can cope, many of them cannot and have to get their partners to deal with cleaning up and holding the baby until the mother feels it is safe to do so again.

As the child gets over the age of one year the problems seem to really start. Babies of this age are starting to mix with other children at toddler groups, mother and baby mornings or even nurseries if the parents are going back to work. Because of this mixing with other children, the incidence of virus transfer suddenly becomes a lot higher. When my eldest son was just a year old he went to a crèche for a couple of hours in the morning a few days a week. The second day after he'd started there, he awoke and threw up all over his bedsheets. He had a raging temperature and looked really pale. I didn't know what to do. I can remember feeling torn between wanting to care for my ill son and staying away from him in case I caught whatever it was he'd got. I was also five months pregnant with twins by then and I didn't want to get sick whilst carrying them either. I'd already been into hospital with contractions, which they'd managed to stop, and if I got a stomach virus what might that set off?

I sat nervously on the couch away from my son who kept holding his arms out to me to be cuddled. He was already being cuddled by his dad but he wanted (like most children) to be with his mother whilst he felt ill. I felt such a bitch. What an awful mother I was being. Turning away from him, denying him the comfort he needed from me, just because I was so scared of him and what he could pass on to me. I hated it. The only thing I could think of to do for him was to take him to the doctor and see if there was some magical medicine that my one-year-old could take that would stop him being sick. My husband had to come too. But there wasn't a magic medicine. Time was the answer, and lots of fluids. I felt so frustrated by my inability to help him that I felt like punching a wall. I wanted to be able to do something, but there was nothing.

It turned out that my son had gastro-enteritis and it lasted four days – four horrible days of my son suffering and of me torturing myself with thoughts about what a useless mother I was. As the vomiting stopped, I forced myself to hold my son, whilst holding my breath and trying to breathe in shallowly through my nose, just in case. These occasions became more and more frequent and I felt better for holding him and comforting him and finally feeding him again. For over a week afterwards I waited to see whether I would get ill, if I would catch what my son had. I ate 'safe foods' such as toast and soups, light foods that wouldn't upset my stomach or make me wonder if I was getting ill or suffering with food poisoning.

I lost three pounds in weight that week. For other emetophobic women and mothers, the weightloss can be worse. The majority of emetophobes are already grossly underweight so losing weight through stress and not eating at such frequent intervals can have terrible side effects for a body that is already nearly running on a constant empty. They get ill. They fret and worry and limit their food intake to 'safe foods' again and the vicious cycle continues. How can it be broken?

When you become a mother, you know that you have many years ahead of you to take care of the children until they are old enough to leave home. Some emet mothers measure this time as how much longer they've got to take care of a child that might get sick. Cold viruses, headaches, influenza and chicken pox can all be dealt with providing they don't make the child vomit. In fact, some emet mothers reported that they welcomed their child getting ill with chicken pox or a cold because then they actually felt they could do something for their child and their son or daughter would then think 'Oh, Mummy does care for me when I'm ill.' Maternal guilt is a huge driving force and something that should never be underestimated.

School

Yet another worry for emetophobic mothers is the fact that most of them end up having to do the school run. Not a big deal, some may say, a good time to share together with your children before they go to school. But for an emet, it is like walking through a nightmare – all those children, all those parents, all those unseen stomach bugs just waiting to sneak up on you without warning. That is how emets think. It's those constant thoughts again. They don't think about the school run per se. They're thinking about whether today will be the day they or their child gets infected with something. They'll stand in the playground with their child listening to everyone's conversations to see who might have been ill the night before. If they do hear someone say that his or her child has been sick with a tummy bug, they will move to another part of the playground, but will keep a careful watch on the previously sick child to make sure he or she doesn't come into contact with their own. An emet mother might even question her child as to whether he or she knows the previously sick one and whether they share a classroom, whether they ever play together, etc.

Unfortunately, sometimes a stomach virus does sweep through the school. On these occasions, emets can react in different ways, depending upon how bad their emetophobia is in the first place. When I hear about a stomach bug going round the school I will instantly feel dismay, then worry, then fright. I will act normally to everyone else, but I'll be breathing very shallowly through my nose, desperate to get away as quickly as possible. I will inform my children to make sure they wash their hands before they eat anything and not to eat any shared food that comes from a bag that has been handed around. For me, that is the best I can do to protect them. Then, of course, I'm watching them (and myself) for any signs of a stomach virus for weeks afterwards. Some other emets have taken more drastic action:

> As soon as I hear there's something going around, that's it. I won't go there until I think it's safe. I've even taken my son out of school for weeks on end because I'm too scared to go, or send him in. I keep expecting to get in trouble with the school or with truant officers, but I don't care. I'd rather stay healthy. (Jackie, 43)

Is this an overreaction? To an emet it certainly isn't. In fact any emets reading this might wish they were as brave as Jackie to stay away from the school and risk the wrath of the authorities. With the winter vomiting virus (also referred to as Norwalk or Norwalk-like virus) hitting the UK harder and harder each year (or so it seems to emets), more and more children of emets are spending time away from school for far longer than is necessary.

I'm sure, right now, you can see why a book on this subject was needed. The implications of emetophobia reach far and wide and extend to those around the sufferer. You can see why trying to explain to someone what emetophobia is, is not simple. It is more than just 'a fear of vomiting and sickness'. At the time of writing this book, the first of the sickness bugs is starting the rounds in schools. The Gut Reaction forum is beginning to get busy with frantic writings from worried emets. This will last for months, months of being 'on edge', frantic, worried, stressed, anxious. Doctors know what sort of physiological damage that can do to the body over a long period of time, but add to those problems the low body weight, the fact that emetophobes will begin to limit their foods or even stop eating altogether because of these viruses over a four- or five-month period and there's no knowing what damage will occur.

Of course, being an emetophobic parent is not just about when your child gets sick or goes to school. Another major worry can be birthday parties. At a child's party, there are generally lots of excited children, dancing and running about after filling themselves with food: cake, chocolate, jelly and ice-cream. Invariably, one of those children will be sick at the party or after going home. For this reason, birthday parties are seen as no-go areas for emets.

Emet mothers can be really upset, physically, by the actual area where the child has been ill. After leaving a spouse or relative to clear up the mess, an emet mother will usually be unable to go near that particular 'spot', even if it a well-used part of a room such as a couch used for watching television. The clothes the child was wearing at the time of the 'event' will have notorious connotations for the mother. She may throw out that item, or after it has been washed push it to the back of a wardrobe to reduce the chances of it being worn again. She may watch the child like a hawk if he or she wears the garment again, convinced that the child will get sick once more. Illogical thoughts, they know that, but they're still enough to terrify an emet mother.

CHAPTER TWELVE

Nights and Sleep

Okay, it's night-time. Easy, you just close your eyes and go to sleep, right? Not so for an emetophobe – night-time can be horrible. Most emets have memories of getting sick during the night as a child. It is these memories and hearing about friends and colleagues who have got sick during the night that reinforce their fear and worry. Because being sick and worrying about being sick is such a huge focus of an emet's day, it is perhaps easy to understand why so many of them then dream about being sick. They fall asleep and graphic images run through their heads of their most feared event. Then they wake up feeling terrified, panicking, thinking 'Well, if I dreamt about it, then that must mean I'm going to be ill.'

The cycle of fear continues. They nibble a bit of toast for breakfast, not the whole slice and definitely not the piece they touched with their fingers. They'll take their anti-emetic tablets and tuck themselves in bed away from the world and shiver and shake and spend hours worrying about when it will strike. They might venture downstairs for something to eat at lunchtime or they might not, but if they do it will be something 'safe' and light – something guaranteed not to upset their stomach any more than is necessary. They will spend their whole day like this, sometimes all the next night too, afraid to go to sleep just because of a dream.

Sometimes the dreams will focus on the feelings of nausea rather than the sickness and sufferers will wake feeling nauseated. They will take this as a sign that their body is telling them they don't feel very well and the cycle described above will then take place. They will spend hours thinking about what it was they ate the day before that could have upset them. What could it be? They were so careful, as always, with what they ate. Perhaps they didn't wash their hands before eating something? This starts an internal vow to wash their hands always no matter what, and if there is no opportunity to wash their hands then they will go without. But, what if it wasn't their fault? What if it was someone else, someone who had a stomach bug and failed to mention it?

These sorts of thoughts go round and round in their heads, never ending, never stopping. It's a constant torture for an emet, not knowing the answers, not knowing the truth. Though what good would knowing the truth do? It wouldn't stop the nausea or sickness. It doesn't stop an emet from thinking it all through. It's a part of the phobia.

For some emets, the fear of what their dreams will bring prevents them from going to sleep. They actually fear going to sleep. They fear the nights. Some emetophobes will take stimulants to try to keep awake, drink endless cups of coffee or keep active. They may manage this for a few nights before the total lack of sleep gets to them and they find themselves napping on and off, usually waking with violent jerks as they suddenly realise they've fallen asleep.

For some emets, it's not just the fear of sleeping but the fear of waking. What if the dream is true? What if they are going to be sick the second they wake up, if they have dreamt it? What about all those stomach viruses that go around that make you sick upon waking? It's simply logical that if you go to sleep you're going to wake up at some point, and what if you wake up and feel ill? Pointless speculation, some might say; utter nightmare, emetophobes would say.

This lack of sleep, the inability to recharge the body by resting, the constant anxiety, the stress and worry can lead some emetophobes to think about suicide. The whole emetophobia experience is just one long turmoil and endless cycle of worry and terror. How can there be an end? Death would seem an attractive end to some. In the Gut Reaction survey (1998) reported on the site, 75 per cent of sufferers say they despair about their phobia; 49 per cent say they feel that it gets worse as time passes; 73 per cent say they are clinically depressed; and a shocking 31 per cent are suicidal: that's almost one third of emetophobes. This is an understandable number to me because the phobia is awful and terrifying and exhausting. Sometimes, it can all get too much and those without the strength to carry on and face it any more could easily feel that dying would be the quick way out of an exhausting existence.

Those emetophobes who do not live on their own, but are perhaps wives or husbands with children, say that because they cannot bear to hear the sounds of possible vomiting or sickness through the night they tend to switch on some kind of background noise to help them sleep and block out any possible illnesses that may occur during the night. This can be the radio tuned into a station, or even the television turned down low. One emet said that she turned the radio to a point in between stations because she thought that her brain would pick up on any references to being sick, or that hearing the DJ cough or clear his throat would scare her.

But what about those emetophobes who don't live with others? Night-time can be a lonely place and for an emetophobe who already lives alone and fears sleeping, dreams or waking, it can be utterly dreadful. It can be a time they use to rearrange bookshelves, scrub down a kitchen or bathroom, or shampoo a carpet – anything but sleeping and realising how horribly alone they are. They may sleep and wake up to find that they feel ill and have no one to turn to but their own sad reflection in the mirror, or perhaps an internet connection.

Sleeping and dreaming raise so many issues for emets. Because so many of these issues are rooted in childhood, for some sufferers they can be quite psychologically damaging.

Events of sickness during the past have usually been relived so often by the sufferer that they have been built up into the worst possible memories, making night-time and waking up during the night feeling ill one of their biggest concerns. Taking stimulants or sleeping tablets is not the answer.

CHAPTER THIRTEEN

Leaving the Home

The safe haven of home – most people think of home as their safe haven, emets more so than anyone else. It is an environment they can control. It is one where they feel safe. They can control who comes in it, what they do in it, what they touch, what they eat. An emetophobe can keep the house spotlessly clean and bleached, knowing that almost all bacteria have been eliminated for that moment, making it safe to prepare some food and eat, for example.

But there come times when sufferers have to leave that safe haven, when they have to go out into an unbleached world, populated by people breathing germs all over the place, touching things with unwashed hands, or even falling ill in the street. For emets, going out brings so much stress and worry because they have to leave their safe cocoon. What might they see? What risk might they expose themselves to? What might they catch without realising it? What if they have a panic attack in public? What if they need a toilet? Before going out, some emets will try to work out how long they will be out for. If it's to go to work, will it be for a full day? If so, where will they eat? What will they eat? Will it be safe? What will they do if they feel sick? Where are the toilets? Are they clean? How long will it take them to get back home?

Is it a shopping trip for food? If so, when would be the best time to go? For an emet a quiet supermarket is the best option, so they tend to shop late in the evening or even during the night, especially if they don't sleep very well.

Have they been invited out by friends? Is it to a pub or club? If it is, then they will probably turn down the invitation. There may be too many drunk people who might be sick, too many people leaning over gutters might be outside.

Is it for a meal? This will most likely be turned down as well, even if it is at a friend's who they know keeps a clean house. The pressure of having everyone watching what they eat will be immense. With most emets being underweight, when they do eat they feel they are being watched, the way overweight people will sometimes say they are watched. If they do go out to eat, what if the food they are served is not considered 'safe'? No, going out causes too many problems even just thinking about it, so they'll come up with some excuse not to go.

Having said that, some emets will try to go out and have a normal life. Even these emets will spend a lot of the time thinking 'How do I feel? Is that meat properly cooked? Oh dear, was that a stomach ache? I need the loo. Where could I go if I got sick?' There would also be a lot of surreptitious clock-watching, as the anxiety builds. They'd be desperate to get back to the safety of their own home where they know that they will feel better.

What if they are asked out to see a film at a cinema? Some emets will not go to cinemas because of the smell of the food and the noise of all those people eating, people who may choke, who may cough. They can't cope with sitting there in the darkness not knowing who they are sitting next to, all those bodies in one room breathing the same air. If they do go, most emets prefer to sit on aisle seats so that they can make a hasty exit without disturbing everyone else or having too many people notice. For the same reason they tend to sit at the back near the exits.

Parties are generally avoided for similar reasons that children's parties are avoided – all that food, all that alcohol. I can personally remember going to a New Year's Eve party thrown by my aunt. I was about 12 and everyone was going and I couldn't be left behind, so I was taken along. I spent most of the evening on the stairs, chatting to my cousin about books. Parties weren't his thing either for some reason. I was aware of a lot of laughing, glasses clinking and bottles being popped open. The adults got louder and louder as the evening wore on and at one point my uncle disappeared through the front door. It turned out he was so drunk on whisky he had thrown up over the garden wall into next-door's goldfish pond. He was gone for ages and when he came back in, looking somewhat the worse for wear, he stank of whisky and vomit.

The stench turned my stomach and I felt awful. I began panicking and then I heard all the adults talking and laughing about next-door's pool and whether the fish were enjoying their free meal. It just made me feel worse and I spent that New Year's Eve and all of the next day in a state of worry in case I got sick. Even though I knew that my uncle had been sick because of alcohol, I still felt there was a small chance that he might have gotten sick because of a bug. Every year after that we were forced to go to my aunt's New Year's Eve party and every year they'd bring up the subject of my uncle and the goldfish pond. It was treated as a huge joke, but to me it wasn't. No one seemed to notice or even care. I learnt to laugh along with them, but inwardly I'd cringe, feel sick and then try to make them change the subject.

One event, years ago when I wasn't even a teenager, was still having repercussions for me years later. Such is the nature of emetophobia. Emetophobes have long memories.

CHAPTER FOURTEEN

Secrecy

Emetophobia is a very secret phobia. Sufferers do not tell anyone how they feel or what they think, for many reasons. I think the first reason is because they think they are the only person in the world who feels the way they do, who has such maddening thoughts. They don't even realise they have a phobia with a real name. They just think it's them and mental health problems. Despite us being in the twenty-first century, they still seem to feel it is something to be feared or hidden away. Sufferers generally wonder, especially at the beginning, if there is something mentally wrong with them. They assume there just has to be because no one else feels the same way, do they?

However, emetophobia is more common than anyone realises. Emetophobia is the fifth most common phobia in the world. Unlike agoraphobia, claustrophobia or arachnophobia, emetophobia is hidden away by sufferers because they feel so ashamed of it. They feel that if they told people exactly how they felt, their friends or family would think they were a little whacko, a little crazy. But surely it can't be right to let your life be so ruled by an extreme fear of sickness and vomiting that it permeates every aspect of it? No, it's not right, but that doesn't mean they have something mentally wrong with them.

Even so, emetophobes are afraid of telling people. They feel they will be made to feel ashamed, will be humiliated or embarrassed. People will use the much over-used refrain of 'Pull yourself together.' If only it were so easy. By the time emetophobes feel that they can actually tell someone how they have been feeling and what sort of thoughts they have on a daily basis, the phobia has usually been with them for years. It's ingrained into their very psyche. It is almost part of who they are. They cannot see where they end and the emetophobia starts. It's almost like they are both part and parcel of each other – without one, there cannot be the other.

Yet emetophobes will sit and wonder for hours what it feels like to be 'normal'; what it feels like not to go through life worrying every second of the day about what they eat, who they'll meet, what it is safe to touch, whether they have washed their hands, whether it's safe to sleep, whether they ought to get pregnant. The list could go on and on. After a while, the whole secrecy aspect of having emetophobia almost becomes part of their shield against the outside world. If they have to pretend to be normal because no one knows they have emetophobia, then everyone will think that they are normal. Only the sufferer knows the whole truth of what is going on. This concealment behaviour may sometimes result in the sufferer freaking out and having a panic attack, leaving friends and family wondering what brought that on, but the event passes and is soon forgotten. The sufferer is not looked upon as somehow being 'weaker' for having a phobia.

There is also an aspect of emetophobia that makes some people laugh. Some phobias are seen by the general public as just being ridiculous, like having a fear of a certain number, or maybe balloons, or perhaps the wind. Why would someone be scared of the wind? These phobics are laughed at. There are jokes made about them and they are even ridiculed on talk shows when they've gone there to try to get some help with their problem. They are willing to finally face the humiliation because the phobia is having such a huge impact on their lives. That is the part that a lot of people forget. A phobic will finally tell usually because it has all gotten too much, but on a talk show it is seen as entertainment – an hour when people can watch and think, 'That person is seriously weird.'

Telling people

Most people would admit to being scared of something irrational. So what is different about being allowed to be scared of something like, say, spiders, yet having a phobia about something is seen as stupid or laughable or something to be ridiculed? Ignorance from others is one of the main reasons why many sufferers don't speak out. Personally, I've had many different reactions from telling people:

- 'She's being ridiculous!'
- 'But why? No one likes being sick. Everyone's like that.'
- 'Emetophobic? What's that?'
- 'Oh, really? Why?'
- 'I used to be like that, but I'm fine now.'
- 'You what?'

Reactions can make a huge difference to how emetophobes would then continue the conversation. If they feel that the listener is not taking the subject seriously, they will try to avert the conversation, no longer wanting to make it a 'big deal'. This person is obviously not ready to hear about it, or not able to understand what the sufferer wanted to confide. If listeners react in a kind way, sufferers may go into a bit more detail about it to try to explain how bad it can be and is, but they won't give the whole story. How could they? It's taking me a long time to write about it. Can you imagine having to say it all?

When I started to tell people I was writing a book about emetophobia, I was pleased by the reactions I got. They wanted to know what the phobia was, how it affected sufferers. I kept the explanations short, but in general, the people I told were those who I knew would listen without scorn. So emetophobes have to be very good judges of character too.

Emets have all sorts of different stories of what happened when they told their friends and family, or spouses and partners. The stories are mixed. Some are nice, others are upsetting and maddening when you hear how some people react.

Another reason that stops emets from telling anybody is the knowledge that, even if they do tell someone else, they feel the other person cannot help them. There is no way that the person being told can help to remove the problem, so the need to actually tell and share the burden of emetophobia is kept contained. It would be interesting to discover if the 31 per cent of emetophobes who are suicidal are the ones who have told many people or not. Is the saying true that a problem shared is a problem halved? If the emetophobe has managed to brave the doctor's surgery and inform the doctor, he or she may be referred to a counsellor. But many emets report that when they do confide their problems to either the doctor or a therapist of any sort, many of these professionals have no idea what emetophobia is. For sufferers, this can be an immense source of frustration. Here they are, having suffered for what may have been many years. They have plucked up the courage to go to the doctor's surgery and told the doctor what is wrong, expecting help, expecting some way that can make their lives easier. Then it turns out that the emet knows more about the condition than the professional.

This in turn has repercussions for other emets who read the message boards on the emetophobia forums, which are sometimes the only places where they can get advice and help. Reading about other emets' experiences, they realise that the professionals may not be able to help and so they don't even bother going to the doctor at all. This is wrong, because obviously the more doctors hear about the condition, the better it is for the next emetophobe who comes into the surgery.

Thankfully, there are some professionals out there who do know about emetophobia. I was lucky enough to encounter one of these when I asked if my son could be referred to a counsellor for his emetophobia. So don't despair, they are out there. This book will also help change matters by informing professionals, teachers, carers, social workers, doctors and other medical professionals just what emetophobia is all about. I think I can end this chapter by quoting from an email I received from another emetophobe who wrote to me about not knowing any other emets. She said, 'I think I may get a T-shirt printed: "Emetophobic? Say hello!"' I thought it was a very good idea indeed.

CHAPTER 15

Releasing the Pressure

By now you, the reader, must have some idea of the amount of pressure an emetophobe feels under every second of every day. Some cope with this constant worry and stress by controlling their diet, exercising, extreme vigilance over the hygiene within their home, whatever it takes to protect themselves from the threat of sickness.

Other emetophobes use a different way of releasing the pressure – self-harm. This harming can be in many forms. One emet confesses to punching herself. Another slaps her legs and thighs and pinches and twists at the skin. Another digs her nail through the flesh until she bleeds. Others admit to cutting themselves regularly with knives, the sight of their own blood somehow creating a release valve for all the pressure within.

I'd always wanted to write this book about emetophobia, but I finally sent out the book proposal after reading a very upsetting confession from a 13-year-old girl who admitted to holding a bread knife against her heart, desperate to plunge it in because she was so fed up with living with emetophobia. She didn't do it. She was too scared of failing. She was not scared of dying but scared of failing and finding herself in a hospital, her worst nightmare, a place filled with unseen bacteria and sick people, coughing and retching around her. She was not scared of the knife or the pain, not scared of upsetting her family, but driven to such a terrifying act by her fear of being sick.

So what drives someone to self-harm? What makes some sufferers think that if they cause themselves pain or cause themselves to bleed the pressure inside them can be released? Is it the visual evidence they need – the blood, the bruising, the scars? Do they actually need to feel the letting of the blood, the trickle? Self-harming emets admit that the release only lasts for a short time. Then they have to do something else, in a different place, again and again until their bodies are a mass of cuts and bruises.

The very act of self-harming is a sign of something deeply distressing going on in a sufferer's life. They self-harm because they very often feel they cannot verbalise the pain or upset they feel inside. It is their way of communicating that something is going on, something that they cannot talk about. Self-harmers have described it as an 'inner scream'. The fear and frustration that emets feel inside can be released through the act of self-harm where the resulting blood or bruising can be seen. The bleeding can be mopped up and bruises salved, yet the fear and frustration are more difficult to alleviate. If they can release it from the body in this way, then they feel they can cope for a little bit longer. If they can get the emotional pain out of their bodies, they can feel distracted by the sight of blood or bodily damage and find some comfort in this way. As they deal with an injury, their minds are off their inner turmoil. By self-harming they also give themselves some control over the phobia, at least for a short while.

In the general psychology of self-harming, most sufferers have gone through some emotional turmoil as a child that was not dealt with at the time. They had no one to confide in, no one they could talk to, no one who would comfort them. This aspect of self-harming has the greatest relevance to emetophobes as research shows that most phobics can base the start of their fear in their childhood. Because that childhood fear did not receive an outlet, adults may begin to self-harm, releasing the emotional fear by cutting or harming their body, turning their anger and frustration and fear upon themselves and keeping the phobia away for a few hours more.

Some self-harmers report that they feel no pain during the act. Their body disassociates from the physical pain, the way it has concentrated uniquely on the emotional pain. Yet emetophobic self-harmers profess to feeling the pain and they like it because it gives them something to concentrate on other than the emetophobia. There are some contact details and addresses for those who self-harm at the end of the book.

Of course, for some emets (31%) suicide is often contemplated as the only way to escape from the fear. Please note that of this percentage most emets said that they 'thought' about suicide, but also knew that they would not go through with such an act. The thoughts are just there, always lurking, like some creature in the shadows, letting them know that there is a way out that is just very horrible to contemplate. They think about suicide, what it means, how they might go about it, but they don't actually do it.

Having said this, there will also be a small minority that do contemplate suicide as a valid way out of the trap of emetophobia. Most comments I have read from sufferers that deal with suicide seem to come from the younger emets, those in the teenage years. Perhaps this is because they have not yet had time to create their own coping strategies to get through each day. But how horrific is that? Imagine not knowing about your child's emetophobia and not knowing that your son or daughter is contemplating suicide because of it. How much better are their lives going to become by making the life of an emetophobe more truly known, by making the suffering more public knowledge? It may not, of course. It may make it worse. However, by educating people about the phobia and how it affects lives in all manner of ways, we can make it easier for emetophobes to be able to say 'I have emetophobia.' They need to know that when they say that there will be people who understand whom they can talk to, people who can give them the coping strategies they need to get through each day rather than contemplating the 'easy' way out.

CHAPTER 16

Emetophobia in Children

Emetophobic parents have a bad time worrying that their child may come home with some sort of stomach virus. Their other main worry is that they will somehow 'pass on' emetophobia to their child/children. Personally, I always thought I'd been very careful. My emetophobia does not bother me too much except when there are bugs going around and my anxiety levels rise greatly. Whenever I felt ill myself and began to feel panicky, I would always go to my bedroom and be on my own. I prefer to be alone when I feel ill. I like to know that there is someone close by if I need them, but generally I prefer to be alone. (I put this quirk down to vomiting in the public swimming baths as a child.) So whenever I got sick I felt that it was okay for me to be in my room because my children wouldn't see how feeling sick affected me. If my children ever came upstairs to see how I was, I would feign being okay, give them a quick hug and a kiss and send them back downstairs – simple.

Yet my eldest son became emetophobic. He's now seven years old, but when he was six he went to his grandparents' house for a sleepover. He had Sunday lunch with everyone and started to feel ill. He was sick at their house and begged his grandparents to call us to bring him home. My husband fetched him whilst I waited anxiously for them to return. I felt so sorry that my son had got ill, but I didn't think too much about it until he started to refuse to eat hot dinners. He said that a hot dinner had made him ill at his grandparents so he wasn't going to eat hot food. For about a month he lived on sandwiches, fruit and breakfast cereal. It was all we could get down him.

A red flag was waving madly in my mind as I recognised this extreme behaviour. Next, he started refusing to go past a certain landmark, a bridge, near our home. He stated that going past this bridge meant he would get sick and any attempts to drive or walk him over it resulted in terrifying panic attacks when he would collapse to the floor and plead with us to let him go back home because he felt so scared of getting sick. As you can imagine, I felt awful for him. I also felt guilty. Had I somehow passed this on to my son? How could it have happened? I'd never been like that in front of him. I'd never told him I was scared of being sick or that it was something to fear, never. Yet here he was showing all the signs.

Next, he decided that just leaving the house would make him get sick and he started refusing to go to school. If I did manage to get him into school, he spent all his time in the medical room hyperventilating, panicking and crying. Then he decided that eating food away from home would make him sick so he stopped eating school dinners too. I gave him packed lunches but he wouldn't touch these either. The school was slightly worried that it would affect him educationally if he had no strength to get through the day and I agreed. Something had to be done. But what?

From personal experience of having many different therapies and counselling that hadn't worked, I was reluctant to ask for my son to be referred to a counsellor. After all, I reasoned, what could they do? As far as I was aware, no one had been cured of emetophobia. Why would a child therapist be any different? But I knew I had to do everything I could for him so I called the health visitor and asked her to refer him. The physical and mental stress was taking its toll on me as well as my son. It was also affecting the other children who wondered what was so scary at school that their older brother didn't want to go.

The first counsellor to see my son was a very confident woman who insisted that she could cure a child of any fear. She spent some time telling me that she'd cured a child of her fear of the wind and another of a fear of dogs; that curing my son would not be a problem. She saw him in school and the main focus of her questioning seemed to be 'What is more scary? Being sick or being stepped on by a giant?' My son thought she was funny. Being stepped on by a giant? That had to be more scary. You'd get squished! You'd be dead. Of course it was scary. The counsellor felt that she'd made progress with this admission and told me that my son would be cured within months; that we'd get him past the bridge easily enough and he'd start eating hot meals again. Unfortunately, after just one session with my son she left through ill health and retired. She informed me that my son would be referred to another counsellor. I felt a little worried by this. Another counsellor? My son already knew her. Would we have to go through the whole story again? The short answer was yes.

The next counsellor, a man this time, called in to say he was my son's new case worker and asked me to tell him a little about the problem as he didn't have any notes. He came to our house to meet with us and promptly said that he knew about emetophobia and there was no point giving my son therapy and getting him to talk about it because no amount of talking would make any difference in this case. The aim was to get my son to get through each day realising that he could cope with what it threw at him.

I was actually quite pleased with what he said. Here was a man who knew what he was talking about because even though talking does help it doesn't 'cure' emetophobia, which was what the first counsellor had thought she could do. The new counsellor was happy to give us some things to talk about and coping strategies for my son to use. We employed them, slowly at first, but they're having results. My son is still emetophobic, but he is not as bad as he used to be. He eats hot meals. He goes to school. He goes past the bridge.

Did I give my son emetophobia? I think not. I did a lot of soul searching on this and I really do believe that he became emetophobic all by himself. Yes, it's a coincidence that his mother has the same phobia, but if I'd shown him how to be scared of being sick then surely my other three children would also have emetophobia? Anxiety and problems with our nerves seems to run on my side of the family. My mother has been on medication for years because of stress and anxiety. I'm a naturally anxious person and my son is too, more so than my other children. Like me he got sick away from home. He didn't feel as if he could talk about it and he felt embarrassed about it happening. Naturally the fear developed in the unique way that emetophobia does.

Seeing your child trying to cope with emetophobia is extremely difficult for a parent. If neither parent has emetophobia, it can be hard to understand. They may get angry and frustrated that their child resorts to some extreme behaviours to keep him- or herself 'safe' from sickness. They may force their child to go out from home, increasing the child's levels of stress and worry and subsequently making the phobia worse.

If they do have emetophobia themselves and then witness it in their children, it can be very upsetting. Most parents want what is best for their children and they certainly want them to have a stress-free, worry-free childhood. To see their children struck down by some terrifying fear that limits their life and stops them going out and enjoying themselves, or even stops them from feeling able to leave the house, can be one of the most worrying and upsetting things for parents to live through.

Letting the child talk is a good thing. Letting children know that they can discuss their fears and anxieties without being laughed at is very important. The earlier and quicker the fear is dealt with, the less of a grip it can have on a child's life. Finding your particular child's strengths is important, as is giving your child some coping strategies to help him or her get through a panic or illness. The important thing, is to do it together. Whether you understand emetophobia or not, do not leave a child to cope with it on his or her own. You do not want your child to be one of those emets who grows up self-harming or feels that suicide is the only way out. You want to know that your child can come and talk to you and for you to give him or her a hug.

CHAPTER SEVENTEEN

Effect of Emetophobia on Non-emets

Living with an emetophobe can be incredibly stressful and in some cases can destroy relationships. Imagine for a moment that you are living with your spouse. You want your future to be together, to grow, to have a family, but your partner – who loves you very much – feels she cannot face a wedding. She couldn't possibly get through a wedding ceremony, never mind a meal afterwards. And as to having children, they might also be out of the question because of the fear of morning sickness. Oh, and what about all those times out you foresaw, of you and your partner having meals in restaurants or going on holiday? Well, they're out of the question too. Would you want to stay with that partner?

In more severe cases of emetophobia where it has such a huge grasp on an emet's life, it can seem understandable why non-emets may choose to walk away. Why should they put their life on hold for something that may never be cured? Why should they put aside their wish for children? Why should they forsake the idea of ever going on a holiday with you, or even a night out, or of ever having a drink? Why should they put up with someone who consistently bleaches everything? Why should they be prevented from kissing their partner or being more intimate with them? It is understandable, when put into those contexts, why some may choose to leave their emetophobic partner.

But what if the emetophobia is not that bad? What if it doesn't have such a grip on both their lives and they have got married and have had children? How does the emetophobia affect them then? I asked a sample of non-emets who were married or living with an emetophobe how the phobia affected their lives. Most stated that they lived essentially normal lives just like everyone else, but it became more apparent that something seemed to be wrong whenever illness was mentioned. Whether it was a child or an emet themselves who'd gotten ill, the non-emet partners stated that they tended to be the ones who were left to do all the caring and clearing up of any messes. They were the ones who spent many sleepless nights constantly getting up to a sick child whilst their partner hid away in another room, or in the car on the driveway.

The non-phobic partners seemed to show that they tried their very hardest to understand the thoughts running through their partner's head, but they really didn't think that being sick was that big a deal; that being sick and vomiting was something that everyone did and no one liked, but sometimes it just happened.

Having to comfort an emetophobic partner seemed to take up an inordinate amount of time, time that they felt should have been spent with just getting on with life or looking after children and comforting them. The majority of non-phobics stated that they often had feelings of anger towards their emetophobic partner, though these thoughts and feelings were fleeting. Occasionally, the frustration of being the one to have to cope would descend into an argument with the emetophobic partner, though these occasions were rare.

The non-emet partners admitted to thinking that they often thought their partners were making 'mountains out of molehills' and that if they just calmed down then they'd be fine. In their opinion, it wasn't the sickness but the anticipation of nausea and the actual panic attacks that made the emetophobia worse each time.

All the non-emet partners and family members I spoke to mentioned the words regret, sympathy and anger. The majority had resigned themselves to living with this condition for the rest of their lives, supporting their anxious partner through times of difficulty and generally hoping that the effects of the phobia would lessen with time. They also seemed to think that if their phobic partner actually did vomit, then the phobia would lessen and their lives would probably get back to normal. Unfortunately, the emets who have actually vomited whilst being in the grip of their phobia have reported that even though the vomiting was not as bad as they'd feared, the phobia did not disappear afterwards. It may have abated for a while and some of them even thought they might be cured, but the phobia, unfortunately, still remained. This is not good news for the non-emets. This phobia, it seems, is simply frustrating for everyone involved, whether they have emetophobia or not.

CHAPTER EIGHTEEN

Counselling and Therapy

When I was 17, my doctor decided that it would be in my best interests if I saw a psychotherapist about my 'problem'. At this point in time my doctor wasn't sure what the root cause of my anxiety was, despite my having told her about the phobia and how it seemed to affect me every day. My stress levels were so high that I was in a period of not wanting to leave the house, preferring to stay within the safe confines of my parents' home, so the psychotherapist agreed to come to me.

When he arrived, he sent my parents into the kitchen so he could talk to me alone. I sat there full of relief that finally I could talk to a professional, someone who would help me out of the nightmare I was in. He would listen. He would know about emetophobia, surely. I talked and cried, cried and talked. When I'd finally spent about an hour sobbing my heart out and hiccuping my way through a frank discussion of how the fear of sickness seemed to control everything I did, the psychotherapist nodded, made some notes and called my parents back in. Then I was sent into the kitchen. I couldn't hear what was being said, but he spoke to my parents for about 15 minutes before I was called back in. His verdict was that I had a fear of food, not vomiting.

I sat there, stunned, as he laid out his theory and couldn't believe what I was hearing. Had I just exhausted myself emotionally for nothing? I wasn't afraid of food, I love food. I'd love to eat more of it, but this man had not understood this. He'd listened to me, then listened to my parents whose sole worry had been about the small amounts of food I ate and how I seemed to worry about certain foods, and had come to the conclusion that I had a fear of food and was a borderline anorexic. Anorexic? Anorexics are afraid of getting fat. They have illusions about how their body appears in the mirror. I wanted to put on weight. I could see how thin I was and hated my skinny ribs and bony limbs.

My opinion of the therapist plummeted like a stone but my parents grabbed on to his diagnosis like a lifeline. Emetophobia they couldn't understand, they'd never heard of it, but anorexia – they knew about that. They could fight that. So they made me another appointment to see the therapist. This time I would go to the hospital to see him. I had to wait about a month. I went to see him and listened for about 45 minutes as he spouted on about increasing my calorie intake each day until I was eating a normal amount. I nodded and listened, too polite to tell him he was wrong. I just never went back to see him again.

Next came hypnotherapy. A lovely lady named Catherine came to the house. She assured me that she could get rid of any phobia through a session of hypnotherapy. She imagined it would take about four to six sessions at a cost of £50 each. Okay – £300 for a cure – I thought it would be worth it, especially after a lifetime's worth of anxiety and stress.

She first showed me how to get into a relaxed state and informed me I could use this technique to meditate every day, which would help with anxiety in general. Then she 'hypnotised' me. She took me back to times in my life when I'd been sick and made me relive them until they weren't so upsetting. We did this over and over again until she brought me out of my meditative state. She did this for six weeks running. Nothing changed.

Then I tried reflexology. Nothing happened.

Next I tried cognitive behaviour therapy (CBT) and again nothing happened. Talking about the past, recounting past events where vomiting had been involved, did nothing to lessen the phobia. I gave up and decided to live with it, as have many others.

There are many emets on the various forum sites who report that therapy and counselling are in themselves helpful to some degree. You talk about your fears, thoughts and worries and sharing the problem usually helps to ease the burden. But no one has reported outright that going for CBT or counselling has cured them of emetophobia. As my son's therapist said, emetophobia can't be talked away.

Having stated this, let me stress that, in my opinion, if you have emetophobia and get referred for counselling or therapy, then you should consider going. It won't cure you, but it sure as hell helps to talk things through and lessen the burden. The therapist can teach you how to relax, maybe even meditate, or how to breathe properly when you have a panic attack. He or she will come up with some coping mechanisms for you to use whenever a panic attack strikes and this information and support are extremely useful.

Of course you should make sure that you feel comfortable with your counsellor or therapist. You have to feel that you can talk to this person. You will be confiding in him or her and you must be able to feel comfortable about that. If you don't feel 'right' with a certain counsellor, then try another until you find one you do like. This may mean having to tell your story all over again, but it gets easier with each telling and, who knows, you may find a great counsellor at your first attempt. Make sure your counsellor is registered with the British Association for Counsellors and Psychotherapy (BACP; see Organisations and online resources, pp.156–7).

Some emets report that after going to counselling for some time and feeling secure about their counsellor's suggestions, they are asked to compile a Challenge List. This can be a list of any number of things that relate to an emetophobe's phobia such as only eating safe foods or not comforting an ill child. Emets are challenged to put the things they fear on this list and to challenge themselves to do one item each month if they feel ready. If they feel they can only eat toast and soup when there is a sickness bug going round, they then have to challenge themselves into eating foods other than those they previously considered safe. If able to do this, they may feel a sense of success and euphoria. They challenged themselves and nothing bad happened. The list can always have more and more things added to it. The technique can be very helpful in containing the emetophobia in one small area. It does not 'cure' but it does help an emetophobe feel more confident and able to get through the day. However, I do recall reading somewhere that one emetophobe put on her list 'Eating undercooked chicken', which was the one thing she never did, quite sensibly, I might add.

Desensitisation seems to be a popular suggestion from professionals as to how to deal with emetophobia. They usually start off by suggesting that the phobic listens to a tape of someone being sick, even taking the tape home to listen to, until the noises don't cause panic. The next step might be to watch a 'vomit video' (though reportedly such videos are notoriously false and complete acting, making emetophobes feel their fear is not being taken seriously, that it is all a joke). Emets are instructed to watch the video until it no longer upsets them. At the next session they may have to sit next to a bowl with some vomit in it, or even be in the room whilst a 'volunteer' comes in and makes him- or herself sick.

This desensitisation really is the most laughable idea. Emets try it because the medical professional suggests it and they are willing to try anything to cure themselves of their phobia, but in reality, it doesn't work at all. In some cases it just reinforces for the sufferer how terrible vomiting and sickness are. Others wonder how on earth they can be desensitized when they suffer desensitisation every day. They cope with nausea and sickness all the time, day in, day out, so how can watching a video help?

CHAPTER NINETEEN

Coping Strategies

We've read of some of the ways in which emetophobia can impact on phobics' lives. We know how much they fear and why they are fearful, but what can they do to help themselves get through each day? Hiding away from life in your own home and only ever going out because you desperately need something is not the way. Life has to be faced up to. Emetophobes should not hide away. This will only make them worse, becoming more controlling over their immediate environment. Because vomiting is such a loss of control over your own body, the temptation to gain as much control as you can elsewhere runs deep, which is why emets have their 'funny little ways'.

Yet emets have to be brave and strong. They have to take deep breaths and step out into the world, challenging themselves to take it as it comes. They will never avoid sickness. It's impossible unless you live in a bubble, and even then I have my doubts. Emetophobes have to accept that they can have a partner and a family; they can travel, eat out and go on holidays; they can go into a school and not have to hold their breath in case they catch something; they can deal with an ill child and comfort it. They just have to be courageous and positive. Some people may sneer at the idea of having to be courageous to do these things. They may think this is just normal life, so why am I making it out to be such a big thing? Because for an emetophobe it's huge, immense, but it can be conquered with confidence and bravery.

The first thing to concentrate on is the panic attacks. Once you've had one panic attack, the fear of having another can make it seem more terrifying. The first one overwhelms you. You hyperventilate, you can't breathe, you get dizzy and sick. You shake and tremble and want to run away from whatever it is that scares you. We need a coping strategy to deal with that. First, accept that you've had a panic attack before and that in all likelihood the chances of it happening again are, at this moment, high. So in a quiet moment try to think back to that first panic attack. Think it through. Try to remember how you felt physically, mentally and emotionally. Analyse it thoroughly and then – and this is the hard part – accept that it was okay to feel that way at the time. You had no coping mechanisms to deal with it and you didn't know what was happening, but this time you will be prepared. It all comes down to the simple act of breathing – yes, breathing. You need to breathe slowly and calmly. Inhale through your nose to the count of three and then exhale to the count of three. Imagine with each inhalation that your body is gathering all its tension together in one place and then, when you exhale, you are releasing that tension.

If you feel a panic attack coming on, try to sit down if you can because pacing the floor like a caged animal will only make it worse. Sit down and try to relax the muscles of your body. You will be fighting the 'flight or fight' instinct as adrenalin courses through your body, but if you slow your breathing and sit still, relaxing your body, you will gradually regain control. As you feel yourself regain control, the nausea will diminish slightly (as panicking makes it worse) and once you have control you can then cope with the next situation.

Then there is the problem of feeling sick. Some emets can go decades without actually being sick. One woman reported that it had been over 50 years since she'd last been sick and, surprisingly, being an emetophobe seems to make you less sick. You feel sick and nauseous, but that's because you're more sensitive to feeling nauseous. You're always alert for it. What a non-emet may take for a muscle pang or nervous feeling, an emetophobe will take as nausea prior to being sick. We're too alert. That's why relaxing (and accepting the inevitable may happen at some point) is key to helping you cope with emetophobia.

So, let's imagine you wake one day and you feel sick. Initially you panic, but let's assume it doesn't become a full blown panic attack because you've been practising relaxation, meditation and deep breathing exercises. What do you do now? You could take a tablet and take to your bed, but I find that this can be one of the worst things you can do. Lying there quivering under your quilt, wondering what's happening to you, can make your mind create some pretty wild thoughts and imaginings. Most emets state quite clearly that the best thing to do when they feel sick is to keep busy, and not just physically. Keeping the mind concentrated on other things can help a great deal. Instead of being focused on how sick you feel and how many stomach cramps you've had in the past hour, instead your mind is focused on doing the latest crossword, reading a book, clearing out a cupboard, or whatever else you've chosen to do. I find sitting down and systematically going through a puzzle book is very good for keeping the mind occupied, but so is sorting out a bookcase or clearing out the kitchen cupboards, the pantry or even (and this is a particular favourite of mine) working on a piece of cross-stitch embroidery.

What about when you're out and about? What can you do to occupy your mind? Well, if you're in a car you could look at the number plate of the car in front and try to think of a word that has all of its letters in it, or use the numbers to create some incredibly difficult piece of maths. Perhap you could look at the scenery, or watch the people in the cars you are passing and try to imagine their names and what they do for work. Do anything that keeps your mind off your stomach. If you have the opportunity to stop at a roadside café then do. Get out and stretch your legs. Get some fresh air and maybe a drink that you know you'll be able to tolerate. Use the toilet, wash your hands, buy a magazine. Just take some time to calm yourself down and get your brain into a frame of mind that allows you to continue your journey.

These strategies can also apply when others are ill. Emetophobes are notorious for panicking at the slightest sign of illness in others. This is the opportunity to think to yourself, 'It's okay. I can deal with this. I don't need to run away.' This is also where challenging yourself as an emetophobe can come into its own. You don't need to have a list. You just find yourself in a situation that previously you would have found disconcerting or frightening and tell yourself you can handle it. Breathe deeply. Be sensible. If you can't cope on the first try and need to leave a situation then do so, but don't feel that you have failed because you didn't. You challenged yourself to *try*.

Next time it will be easier, or so you'll hope, but you must persevere. Don't ever back off thinking it's all too much. Eat a proper meal, order something you normally wouldn't from a restaurant menu, go to the cinema and sit in the centre of the room. These are simple, small, baby steps, but baby steps lead to giant ones. It will not cure you, but it will make you more confident and able to cope with everything.

CHAPTER TWENTY

Summary

Emetophobia is life-encompassing. It's scary and terrifying and some people think that perhaps taking their lives might be the only way out. They restrict themselves to lonely lives, without having people close, or getting married, or having children. Emetophobia is not something that just affects sufferers when they feel ill. It's every second, every minute, hour, day, week, month, year. It interferes with every aspect of a phobic's life and causes depression, anxiety, OCDs and other phobias.

This book was written to raise awareness in everyone. Right now, it may be the fifth most common phobia, but no one seems to know much about it. I want to change that. I want every emetophobe out there to get help. I don't want them cutting themselves or to hear that they're suicidal. I don't want them shutting themselves away in their homes, spending hours each day bleaching surfaces and surviving on a limited diet of toast and crisps. I don't want them feeling that they're all alone in this and that no one understands. I want emetophobes to be able to tell their doctor what is wrong with them and have that doctor nod in understanding and not ask, 'What is that?' I want there to be support systems for emetophobes and not just forums on websites. There ought to be support groups across each country, across the globe, for everyone who needs it. I want to raise awareness. I want to educate everyone about emetophobia.

None of the stories in this book has been exaggerated. They've been written word for word as told to me. The relief to finally tell someone about their fears caused some people to cry and weep, but they all stated afterwards that they felt very cleansed by doing so, that it was cathartic to tell all. I'm not naive. I know that there will still be people who feel unable to tell their loved ones about their emetophobia for fear of ridicule or some other reason. I know that there will still be people who sneer, giggle and make jokes, but those people aren't important. They'll just remain ignorant because that is what they can be labelled if they want to ignore someone's suffering. This is what emetophobia is – suffering, fear, terror.

I hope that, after reading this book, whoever you are, you will put it down feeling that you have gained some knowledge and that you will know how to deal with someone who tells you that he or she is emetophobic. You will be sympathetic but will show support because emetophobes don't want pity or ridicule. They just want help. Let's give that to them.

CHAPTER TWENTY-ONE

Personal Stories from Emets

Fiona

I'm 43. I've had emetophobia since I was 18 months old. I had whooping cough, and although I got over the illness, I was sick every day for over a year. (I've since heard that it's quite common to develop emetophobia after whooping cough.) It amazes me that something I can't even remember has had such a profound effect on my life. I've never known what it's like not to have this fear.

Emetophobia has been with me every day of my life. I had measles when I was three, and I can remember screaming the place down with fear that it might make me sick. My fear of seeing other people being sick is just as bad – in fact, I'd say it was slightly worse because you never know when other people are going to do it. I was watching a sit-com when I was about seven, and one of the characters leaned over a basin with a towel over his head. (Many years later, I realised he had a cold.) I bolted out of the room!

I've always had my family's support. To them, my emet is as much a part of me as my eye colour. I was staying with my aunt and uncle once, when my cousin suddenly vomited. I curled into a ball, screaming that I wanted to go home. They took me without a fuss!

Things aren't any better as an adult. I had a few years in my early twenties when it wasn't the biggest thing in my mind. Then my nieces came along, with all their tummy bugs and I was off again.

I met my partner when I was 26 and he has been tremendously supportive. I've found that to be the case with most people. I've always found it easy to be open about my emet. I want my friends to know why I'm running away!

I didn't have my first baby till I was 36. I kept putting it off because I wasn't sure if I could handle sick kids! (I was never worried about morning sickness – none of the women in my family have had it.) My second son was unplanned. More than one sick child at a time? Yuk! They are now seven and two and I love them more than life. But every minute of every day I worry about when they'll be sick again. My partner works nights at the moment, and it's torture. I dread nights the most. Many times in my teens, I wouldn't fall asleep till dawn.

Viruses are what I fear most, especially now I have children. The fear has multiplied since 2001, when reports of Norovirus outbreaks began to appear regularly in the news. I've been on high alert ever since. My partner once drove 300 miles to get home because our oldest son had a bug. When I hear of an outbreak in my area, I go into starvation mode, eating only the bare minimum I need to keep going. I spent the whole of last December shaky and weeping because it seemed like *everyone* was infected. I dread my son returning from school in case he brings something back with him. I nearly cried with joy one time he complained of feeling dodgy and it was only chickenpox!

I absolutely dread the thought of my sons becoming emets. I try my hardest not to show my fear and, touch wood, they are quite laid back about it. I envy them so much! I hate this phobia, *hate it*! I envy all those people (including my partner) for whom vomiting is just another bodily function. When I imagine what a world would be like where nobody ever vomited, I can actually feel my spirits soaring – just like lottery winners must feel when they see their numbers come up. I wish I could be frightened of snakes or heights. With something like that, you're safe behind your own front door. But emet is *always* with you.

I've never sought help. I honestly don't think it would work. I'm embarrassed to go to my doctor (and I'd have to sit in his germy waiting room). Exposure therapy wouldn't work for me. It certainly doesn't work when my sons are sick.

My life would be so different without emet. I'd have had more children. I would probably have gone into nursing. I'd be a damn sight happier all round. Of all the phobias, this must be the most debilitating, the most soul-destroying. And most people don't understand it. Because, hey, nobody *likes* being sick! Well, I don't just 'not like' it. It's scarier than death.

Melanie

I think when an emetophobic woman decides to have children, that is a strong message or desire that the urge to move life forward, to do what other people do, is greater than the fear. First you have to face the nausea and possible vomiting associated with pregnancy and labour, and then face the host of bugs the children will get.

For me, my job was flexible enough to 'give in' to the morning sickness by staying at home for the duration. It was harder with the second child because I had to look after the first. In a strange way I still find hard to explain, the phobia went into a sort of remission until the time my first child was about one. I was delighted with her, with my husband and job, and because nobody was ill, it wasn't something I had to think about. I have had periods of total remission, particularly in my late twenties. I sometimes drank to the point of sickness, I ate 'high risk' foods and got food poisoning. I still got terribly upset and nervous when I vomited, but it didn't stop me doing things that might be risky.

When my daughter was one, my aunt came to visit and was ill with a stomach bug. We all got ill in turn, and what really threw me was the feeling that I could not look after my daughter when I was ill. This terrified me. I had never thought about it. Other mums said, 'Oh, you just chuck up and carry on with things' but I felt so drained and vulnerable and I think this episode set me off into a neurotic 'what if' mindset.

I explained my fears to my GP, who was very kind and prescribed me a refillable prescription of Stemetil, which I had taken before. But the fear generalised into a sort of high functioning agoraphobia and depression, so I needed anti-anxiety agents and antidepressants as well. All of these things helped. I had a few courses of CBT, but though I understood and agreed with the theory, I could not seem to train my mind to think the right kind of thoughts.

My next pregnancy was not planned, so I found that stressful. I was not on medication at the time but I did not feel right. I had a lovely son when my daughter was two and a half, and I would say though he was an 'easy' baby I was not a natural, easygoing mum and my mind was too busy with work, with fears, and so on. What I did manage to do, or so I thought, was to hide the phobia from my children. When they were ill, I did what all mums do, which was to clean up, cuddle and comfort. This was very, very, very hard and with the wisdom of hindsight, children are more intuitive than we think, and certainly my daughter picked up on some sort of feeling. In the days following one of their bugs, I would more or less stop eating, and of course this weakened my immunity. It also just didn't work. The few times I did pick up bugs from them, I would be sick even if there was very little in my stomach.

Around about the time my daughter was six or seven, I started to notice how much she would panic when she was sick. She was often ill in the car (we haven't had a car now for years: it just became hellish to go anywhere by car) and when she had a bug she would cry and pace the room and have all these little tics. She kept asking 'Will I be sick?' As she has gotten older, her phobia has increased along with general anxiety and reluctance to travel far from home. She is seeing someone in CAMHS [Children and Adolescent Mental Health Services] for the general anxiety but they do not have a handle on the emetophobia or play it down.

I would like to think by telling my daughter the right way to think, the normal way to be, that somehow I can train myself to think that way as well, that it is really no big deal. But I cannot do it for myself, and I feel, um, not terribly optimistic that she will get a grip on it. She is a very, very anxious person. My son, on the other hand, appears fine. So I am left to wonder, nature or nurture? In the main, I blame myself.

Carrie

Looking back, it feels as if I've had this phobia all my life. It's hard to remember a time when I didn't have the same thoughts running through my head. Will I catch something today? Will I see somebody being sick and not be able to get away? But if I think logically about it, I think the root of this fear stems from my primary school experiences.

From the age of about six or seven I was bullied by a gang of boys in my class. They would push me over, twist my arms and do anything they could get away with in the 20 minutes of break time we had. This carried on until I was nine and during that period I went to school every day terrified that I was going to be hurt again. On the worst days I would walk into school sobbing and not stop until I was picked up at the end of the day. The stress of feeling constantly scared and hiding it from everyone was too much for me and whenever I felt anxious I felt sick. At one point I would go to the school office every day and get my mum to pick me up, crying that I didn't want to be sick because I knew it would kill me. Eventually she stopped letting me come home and I was trapped.

I finally got out of that school when I was nine and came home with a black eye and no explanation for it, but at that point my phobia was growing thick and fast. My mind had made the connection between feeling sick and feeling terrified and the smallest incidents could set it off. One of the key moments in the progression of my phobia was in Year 4 when I went to a special assembly for our head teacher. I was preoccupied and not listening, so I didn't hear what the head was saying and didn't know that it was a leaving assembly for him. When he suddenly paused to ask a small boy in the front row why he was crying and the boy responded by vomiting all over the floor, I was petrified. Everyone around him seemed to be panicking and started backing away. We all had to file out of the room and the boy was carried away crying. The whole mood in the hall was one of chaos and urgency and it scared me so much. That was the last day of term and when I came back after the holidays to find my teacher gone, I was convinced it was because that boy had been sick on his shoes.

After that my emet was fully established. I was absolutely terrified of anyone who said they felt ill and would avoid them for days at a time. It didn't help that there was a boy in my class who could vomit at will and used to do it in front of me to scare me. I've lost track of the number of break and lunchtimes I spent crying in the girls' toilets and praying he wouldn't find me. This continued on into my secondary school where once again I was bullied and moved away.

Today I feel I've made some progress with this fear but it's so hard not to let your life revolve around it. All your priorities change when you live with a phobia like this. I force myself to go to school and work no matter how bad I feel because I have to save up my sick days for times when there are bugs going round, or to avoid school trips to risky areas like theme parks or hospitals. I've always wanted to be a teacher, but it's only recently that I've started to see it as a genuine career possibility whereas before all I could do was think about how often small kids throw up.

Every day feels like something that has to be survived, rather than something to be enjoyed. Fun activities are tainted by the constant voice in my mind telling me that my worst fear could be waiting to face me around any corner. This phobia makes life so much harder to live through, and it's hard not to spend every day just wishing that I could be 'normal'. But I'm slowly learning that it's up to me to make the change, to get rid of this thing that wants to ruin my life, and one day I hope I will.

Lynn

I was four years old and in the toilet at school, crying my eyes out. I felt sick, I was terrified, I remember shouting at one of the other children to go and get a teacher. Why I was so scared I don't know, I just wanted my mum. One of the boys in my class had something wrong with him, he was always sick, and he always chose to sit next to me. One time he was ill right next to me. I ran. I have always had this fear of vomiting, of myself and others vomiting, since, well since I can remember, three, four years old. What caused it? Who knows. Could it have been the child in my class who was always sick? Could it be my dad who forced me to eat my dinners until I retched, and came home some nights drunk, ending up in the toilet making a right old noise about it? Could it be the time that my mum's friend brought her baby round, and it was projectile sick across the front room? I ran into the garden hysterical, five years old. Why on earth was I so petrified?

And so it continued, with me not knowing what the hell was wrong with me. Through junior school, if a child was ill, you would find me sitting in a corner somewhere shaking and crying. I would run out of assembly, just hating the fact I was sitting in the middle of a crowd of people and I could be sick in front of them all. Of course I was far too young to explain to the teachers what I was running from; at that young age I didn't even really know myself. Luckily I wasn't a sickly child, I was ill I think once, nothing too dramatic. I was with my nan, who was so loving and understanding. There have been no traumatic vomiting experiences that could have triggered this fear, unless, once stated by a psychiatrist, I have pushed some horrendous traumatic experience to the back of my mind, never to be thought of again. But I have had many a conversation with my mum, and as far as she remembers there have been no traumatic experiences with me and sickness. I avoided going to kids' parties (I still do, I was brave and had one for my son three years ago). One time one of my mum's friends took me to this party. I was about six. I tagged along behind and then ran and hid. I hid for the whole length of this party, in an alleyway, then casually walked home as if I had been and had a great time. I wasn't even missed, maybe that's when all the pretence started.

Secondary school, I hated eating in the canteen. Chips and cheese was my diet for most of my school life. I still hated assembly every morning. I would run out halfway through, making myself the centre of attention. I was so embarrassed, with the other kids and teachers asking me, why do you run out? I didn't know, I knew I hated crowds, I knew I kept getting this absolute wave of nausea come over me and all I could do was run. Why was I so different to everyone else? Why didn't my mum or teachers see that there was something upsetting me? Why wasn't something done to help me then?

I didn't know I had emetophobia, I don't think I even knew what I was afraid of, I just carried on being scared of everything. I didn't go out and party with friends. I had a few experiences with alcohol, but one time was sick in a taxi. I made the taxi driver hold my hand, and never touched alcohol in large proportions ever again. I wouldn't travel too far from home. I thought I would grow out of it.

I was 23 and my brother invested in a computer with 'the internet'. Wow, maybe I could do some research and find out what was wrong with me. So I think I typed in 'scared of sick'. 'Emetophobia is an irrational or excessive fear of vomiting.' I was speechless, it opened a whole new world to me. I was not the only one. I sat there and read the stories of others and I just could not believe I was not the only one. I sat there with tears streaming down my face at the relief that it had a name, like so many hundreds of other people do when they find out they are not freaks after all. Then there was a kind of despair: there was no cure, just people desperate for a cure. There has to be, surely I won't spend the rest of my life with this?

So then began the hunt for 'a cure'. First was a hypnotherapist. Oh yes, of course he'd heard of it, he can cure me in ten sessions at £40 a session. So we spent the first three sessions with me with my eyes closed talking about my very happy childhood, nope, not one bad memory, only when he was sick, and she was sick and I was sick. He was stumped, I could tell he didn't know what the next step was. I mentioned that my dad was strict and made me eat my dinners, so the hypnotherapist decided to focus on the fact that I was probably abused as a child and have blocked out the memories. My dad was strict but I was in no way, shape or form ever abused by anybody. And the emetophobia was in full swing long before my dad made me eat all my dinners. The psychiatrist would not listen to me.

Then there was cognitive behavioural therapy. I was very optimistic and went in with eyes open. The second session I walked in and the therapist had put a bucket of what looked like sick, looking back now it was just a bit of old food, next to his chair. He casually asked 'What's in there?' Well I peered over and then absolutely freaked out, waterworks, shakes, panics, the whole thing. He managed to calm me down and my anxiety levels were pretty low by the end of the session. As I left the room he said, the next session you *will* be making yourself sick in a bucket. I never went back.

I then spent £160 on two sessions with a 'celebrity' neuro-linguistic programming hypnotherapist who also claimed to have the 'cure'. She gave me a 20-minute tape about a secret garden, great, that helped, not. She just stuck another few hundred in her bank account, another poor sufferer taken advantage of.

Then there was a very nice NLP counsellor, very young and inexperienced, didn't have a clue. I knew far, far more than him about mental health problems, I've had years of experience after all (yes I consider emetophobia to be a mental problem). He ended up treating me for agoraphobia. I do not have agoraphobia. I am not scared of going out, I am not scared of crowds, I am not shy, I am not frightened of flying, I am not scared of sailing, I am however scared of being sick whilst being in these situations. Is it so difficult to understand? So he gave me some going out exercises to do, walk ten yards, go back home, the next day walk 50 yards, go back home. I give up!

Finally I decided on the one thing I wanted to avoid at all costs, medication. I went on Zoloft ('Zoloft is well tolerated and effective for the treatment of depression and certain types of anxiety disorders') for one week. That was one of the worst weeks of my life. (The worst was when both my sons and I had gastric flu at the same time, they had top end, I had bottom end, my God, what an absolute living nightmare.) Well, Zoloft basically turned me in to a zombie, my hands were burning, my jaw would tremor violently, I would wake up in the early hours of the morning retching. I was so spaced out I couldn't even talk to people. I will never, ever touch medication again for the rest of my life. If I had continued with the medication, as the doctor advised, I would not be here today, I can promise you that.

It took a while to accept that there is no cure. Acceptance was the biggest favour I did for myself. I have to make the best out of a bad deal. I started telling people about this, why should I feel so alone? This is nothing to be ashamed of. This is me, it's a burden but there's not much I can do about it. Non-sufferers do not understand, nobody likes being sick after all, how many times have I heard that? Okay, let's put it this way, say in the future, God forbid, I was diagnosed with cancer, I would rather die than have chemotherapy and risk that I will be sick. Understand how much I 'don't like it' now? People say I should think about my children, how selfish of me. They would not think I was selfish if they saw how much fear and anxiety I was living with day in, day out, year after year. Yes, every single minute of my day is spent thinking about being sick. I have nightmares about people being sick over me. It is very rare that I don't wake at night and panic about the reason why I have woken, do I feel sick? I can't even escape from the constant nagging thoughts through sleep.

I am scared of being sick alone. I am scared of others being sick, and scared of myself being sick even if someone is caring for me. When my kids are ill I run, they pretty much take care of themselves. After they have been sick I do not want to go anywhere near them for about four days in case I catch something, and I also more or less starve myself in case it's too late and I have caught something. Then, if I am likely to be sick nothing will come up.

The times I have been ill have been absolutely terrifying. The whole time I chant, 'I want to die, I want to die.' Of course being sick isn't all that bad, and afterwards it's euphoria that you actually survived to tell the tale. Maybe because you got through it you are a little cured? Like hell are you, it's just another video memory that you can replay day after day, just add it to the collection of 'horror videos to watch when anxious'.

I do eat takeaways, but usually spend the next 24 hours analysing how I feel, just in case it was dodgy. I am not particularly hygienic, I do not scrub all surfaces or bleach anything that can be bleached. I make a concerted effort not to be like that. If I started on the cleanliness OCD then I don't know where it would end. At least I can hide what I am feeling inside as there aren't many obvious signs that I am a sufferer. My suffering is in my head, it does not manifest itself physically. I'm fab at hiding it. When I tell people they always reply with, 'But you look so "normal".' Don't you just love that? So not only do I have to suffer this, I now have to be looked upon as abnormal because I suffer it. I make myself do things that many emets won't consider: long car journeys, Indian meals, eating out, cleaning the loo without gloves (!!), roller coasters, just so I can live a fairly 'normal' life. But there are also many things I won't do, boat trips, planes, drink alcohol, go out too far alone, go out at all if my stomach is making 'odd' noises.

So where do I stand right now and what does the future hold for me? I have given up on therapy, I have accepted there is no cure. I live each day scared that today might be the day I am sick. I do think about ending it all. I am terrified of growing old and losing the people who 'care' for me, I do not want to end up 70 or 80 years old, alone and petrified. I do not want to be a burden to my boys. My days are consumed with my fears for the future, as if it isn't enough being consumed with thoughts about how I am going to get through the day without any possibility of throwing up. I do have very happy times, but they are always, always clouded by emetophobia. I can't imagine what my life would be like without this. I can't imagine what I would have achieved with my life if I didn't have this. Not being able to fulfil your dreams because you are scared of being sick. You'd have to be here to believe it. I work from home, I internet shop, I have maybe one friend and my family are what keep me going, for now. I live each day praying that one day I will wake up and the fear will be gone, I would give any of my limbs to experience a life of freedom, without fear. For now I carry on 'normal' on the outside, lovely, confident, happy Lynn, but living a nightmare on the inside.

Emetophobia is now recognised as about the fourth most common phobia. There are thousands on the website message boards pleading for a cure, help and advice. I have yet to meet a fellow sufferer in person even though I know they're out there, and probably not too far away. I think I may get a T-shirt printed: 'Emetophobic? Say hello!' How apt, my spellcheck doesn't recognise the word 'emetophobic'.

Jackie

I can always remember when I was small that I hated being sick. Even if one of my brothers or sister were ill I would try and avoid being near them, and I would try and stay at a friend's house just so I didn't have to be around or near them! I hated being sick, even at such a young age. I don't know when or how it started, but I can remember avoiding the situation whenever I could.

One time I can remember I ate a red ice lolly, and later on I was sick, not a lot, just the lolly I think, but to this day I will not eat a red ice lolly – you know, just in case!

As I got older I used to go out to nightclubs with my mates, but I always used to keep an eye out for anyone that might start to be sick and I often left well before they closed just so I could get home before all the drunk people started to come out...again avoiding the situation!

Life went on and I met my husband Kev. The only thing with Kev is that he came along with five children. I went from being single to having a ready-made family! The kids lived with their mum; we had them every other weekend and every Thursday. As you can imagine there were many moments when I thought about them being sick, which being kids they were, and if 'it' happened and they had been at home they had to stay there as I couldn't have them in the house, or if it happened when they were at our house, I would let Kev deal with it and I would stay in our bedroom and sit with my fingers in my ears and basically just freak out and cry (although I never let the kids know) and then the next day as soon as they had gone home (which was a.s.a.p.) I would do all the usual stuff like bleaching the house from top to bottom; I would wash all the bedding, towels and anything else that needed it! And then I would do the usual and starve myself and worry for three days in case I had got whatever it was that they had.

I had never wanted children, mainly because of the morning sickness but also when the child is sick, I knew that I would never be able to cope with it. But as time went by and Kev's kids (my now stepchildren) had got older I started to think that I wanted a baby and so did Kev. All the thoughts of sickness went out of my head at that time because I wanted a baby so much, and after seven months of trying I did a test and found out I was pregnant. I was over the moon, phoned everyone I knew and spread the news, I was so happy... Then that's when the thought hit me...*Oh my God* I am pregnant, what if I get morning sickness? How will I cope?

I was okay for a couple of weeks, and then it started. I felt so nauseous every morning, I just didn't know how I was going to cope, and then it went on that it wasn't just in the morning, it was almost all day, but I never threw up, felt like I was going to many times, but thank God I never did. I didn't eat a lot and never had any cravings, if anything I went off certain foods, just the thought of eating chicken made me feel even worse.

As the pregnancy went on the sickness feeling went away, and I started to enjoy being pregnant. I had a few complications and had to stay in hospital for a couple of weeks, and I had a room to myself so that was okay.

After Scott was born I just enjoyed being a mum. I coped fine, even when he was sick because it was only baby sick and it was just milk, but the thought was always at the back of my mind how was I going to cope when he did it and it was proper sick. My mum and everyone else kept on telling me that when it is your own child you cope.

One night it happened. Kev and I were sitting downstairs when we heard Scott let a scream out, and at that moment I knew it was going to happen, I don't know how I knew, I just did. He was 18 months old so we also had the baby monitor on. I was halfway up the stairs when I heard him doing it. I shouted for

Kev, but at the same time I went into his room, picked him up out of his cot and took him into our room and took his clothes off, while Kev sorted out the mess. I don't know why but I just did it, and I felt so proud that I had done that. I even remember saying to Kev, 'I done it Kev, I have changed him and I am with him.' I was so happy that I had just done it and not ran away!

After that for a while I wasn't worrying about all the what ifs and what would I do when it happens. I have done it once and I could do it again. Life went on as normal. Kev was a driver and often his work would take him into Europe; sometimes for four to five days at a time. I often felt alone; although I had Scott, I missed Kev, but got on with life.

One time Kev got called away and it was about 1 am when I heard Scott in his room. He was crying. Straightaway I knew it wasn't the normal crying. I knew what was about to happen. I got out of bed and went into his room and there he was in his cot and he just threw up. It didn't go over him which was okay because that meant I could grab him out of his cot, shut the door and take him downstairs. I plonked him down and phoned Kev. I don't now why I phoned him because there was nothing he could do! I then phoned my mum, but she didn't hear the phone, so I phoned my stepmum, and after babbling to her she said she was on her way. While I was waiting for her to come Scott started to cry again. I knew he was going to be sick, so I took him to the front door and opened it (it was freezing) and told him he would feel better in a minute. Poor thing, he was feeling so poorly and all I could do was be in a state of panic, although I tried very hard not to let Scott see what a mess I was. I just felt I was letting him down because what I should have been doing was have him on my lap with a bowl and comforting him and telling him he would be better soon, but I couldn't do that, and the guilt still eats away at me for the times I haven't been able to do that! Anyway, he was sick again. I had just put a towel on the floor and let him do it on there because it meant I could just cover it and throw it away. My stepmum arrived and took over, she stayed with him until Kev arrived home the next morning. I stayed in the room with them, but each time he was going to be sick I went in the kitchen and blocked my ears. How bad is that? I just felt such a bad mum! Then something happened. As soon as Scott went to bed I found I just got into a panic, I couldn't stay in the house, because every time Scott was sick it happened at night. I started to stay at my mother-in-law's house. She knew about my phobia. Although she couldn't quite understand it, she let me stay there. I would put Scott to bed and then leave Kev with him. I would get up early and get back there before Scott woke up so I could be there when he woke and he wouldn't know I hadn't been there! I did this for about a week, and then I thought I really should be at home, also it wasn't fair on Kev. He was okay with it because he knew what a state I would get myself into. The first night I was at home at night was very hard for me, every little noise Scott would make, even if he just turned over I would be convinced that this is it, he is going to be sick! It was a real nightmare for me just to stay there, but I did.

Things got back to normal once again (that is until I got past the stage where I knew I wasn't going to catch whatever it was that Scott had!). Kev didn't go into Europe with work, he just did the UK stuff for a while because I couldn't cope with being on my own with Scott at night. I was okay in the day because there was always someone I could run to if I needed to.

After a few months, near Christmas time, Kev said he was going to pop to Calais to get some stuff for Christmas. I said I was okay with that. He planned to go on the Tuesday. He was going at night so he would be back in the morning for work, but some time through the day he said he couldn't be bothered to go and would go the next day. So on Wednesday evening he set off. Everything was okay, until at about 2 am I heard Scott do that 'cry', and I though oh my God, this cannot be happening yet again. Kev hadn't been away for ages and now he has gone he was going to be sick *again*, this can not be happening, plus the fact that Kev had changed the night he was going, *why* was this happening to me?

I went in to Scott, I couldn't just leave him. I got him out of bed and he started to heave, so I stood with him. I was holding him from behind and he threw up all over the carpet. I remember thinking briefly as we went out of his room that he will never have spaghetti hoops again! Funny what thoughts go through your head at a time like that eh! I then phoned Kev, he couldn't believe it either. I then put Scott in the car and took him to my mum's, she lived ten miles away. I must have done almost 100 mph, I didn't care if the police stopped me, at the time I just needed to get Scott to my mum's house before he was sick again! I knocked on the door, explained what had happened and handed him over and went out and got in my car. The feelings I had about being a bad mum was unreal. Here was my little boy, who is my world, I love him to bits, but at the one time he needed his mum, I mean really really needed me, I couldn't be there for him, I had dumped him and left! I didn't go home, I drove the car to a layby and stayed there. I couldn't go home because there was vomit on the carpet! I waited until morning and then went back to my mum's. Scott was okay by then. She said he had been sick a few times but was okay now. I put him in the car and drove home. As we got there Kev was back, he had cleaned up. The feelings I had about being a failure as a mum were unreal. But after that it happened again, when it came to Scott going to bed I went off to my mother-in-law's again! I just couldn't be in the house. I felt almost relieved when it was bedtime because I could finally relax, and as it was Christmas time my mother-in-law was staying at our house, so I had her house to myself. The relief I felt when I was there was fantastic. I didn't have to worry about if Scott was going to be sick, I could just be me, I would watch TV and not worry at all. Although saying that, I did miss Kev. I hated the fact that I had to run away and leave him and Scott on their own (with his mum there too). There must have been times when Kev must have thought I was a mad cow! But then saying that the guilt I was feeling was overwhelming!

I remember I was not interested in Christmas at all, I didn't even wrap Scott's presents up until Christmas Eve, and I remember doing it while I was crying. I felt so sad that I was like this, I should have been enjoying wrapping his presents up, but I just wasn't looking forward to Christmas at all.

Christmas morning arrived, and I remember Scott came in our room and I hadn't even taken some of his presents downstairs (how bad is that!) and he started to open some stuff, and I was at the time eating some twiglets (I am a Marmite fan) and Scott wanted one, so I let him have one. He then started to choke on the damn thing, so that set me off. He was okay, but the look of horror on his face will stay with me until the day I die, he looked so worried that I was crying and in a right state, he thought it was all his fault. I calmed myself down, gave him a hug and we went downstairs to open the rest of his stuff. We were meeting with family for a meal out, so that was okay because when we got there I just passed him off to my mum!

Christmas came and went. I was still staying at my mother-in-law's as soon as Scott went to bed. She went back after Boxing Day, so I was there with her in the evenings. New Year's Eve I went to my mum's and poor Kev was at home on his own. I felt so sad that we were not together; I was crying as it turned midnight, I just so wanted to be with him.

After that I made myself go home once again, and after a while things got back to normal again, although it didn't stop me from worrying every night that Scott was going to be sick as soon as he went to bed. That's when I started to do something else – I didn't put him to bed, I used to nestle him down on the sofa with a pillow and blanket and there he would stay until we went to bed. For some reason I was okay with that, and by the time we went to bed I was tired and went to sleep. I know this was not the ideal situation for Scott, but he just fell asleep and Kev would carry him to bed when we went up. For some reason if Scott was in bed I would have to be upstairs too, I couldn't stay downstairs if he was in bed. The thought of him being on his own if he was to be sick was freaking me out. That's where I am sure at some point in my life I must have been on my own when I was sick as a child because why else would I worry about if Scott was sick and alone? I know most people don't like to be around their kids when they actually vomit, but it has turned around for me, I have to be there. Why? I hate it, I hate seeing it happen and I hate everything about it, but I have to be there! Just a mother thing maybe?

I would have loved to have been able to give Scott a brother or sister but just the thought of having another child being sick terrified me so much that I never did. I really admire other emets out there who have more than one child.

As time went on Kev and I decided that we would like to move. We had always liked Hayling Island, as my mum had once lived there, so we sold our house and found one there. But a day before we were due to move Scott was sick in the night (I was blaming it on some custard he had ate). Kev was there, so that was okay, although I had to be with him as he was sick. How odd is that! Anyway, I just thought he would be okay in the morning, but about 6 am he was still being sick and had really bad diarrhoea. What a nightmare situation this was. We were due to move that day and here was Scott so ill. My mum came over to look after Scott while we packed the last of the stuff. The washing machine was going to be the last as we were washing all the last stuff that Scott had been sick on! I was at my wit's end. We had just over a 100-mile drive, Kev was going to be in the lorry driving it, so I would have my dad in the car with me (because he was driving the lorry back to Oxford) and also we had five cats we had to have in the car too!

Anyway, time came and we made it down to Hayling Island. Scott was okay on the journey, but it didn't stop me from worrying and freaking out on the inside all the way down. The next day Scott still had serious bad diarrhoea, but he was happy in himself, he had stopped being sick, so that was good. We settled in okay, but then I thought, Oh my God, I am alone, I don't have anyone I can run to, although I knew this when we moved here. That's another reason we moved – so that I would have to deal with things, not run away from them.

We settled in and made many friends, always good when you have a child because you get involved in toddler groups etc! Scott started pre-school, and that's when I thought I can't protect him any more, he is going to get germs, he is going to eat food without washing his hands etc.!

As you know there is always a bug going around a school. So as soon as I heard of one he wouldn't go to school, as simple as that! I would keep him at home. That was okay while he was at pre-school, but when he was in infants that was different. I used to keep him off too many times and almost got into trouble because he had so many days off, but how could I explain about my phobia to them? They wouldn't understand.

Time passed by, and yes Scott did get bugs from school. Kev was here to deal with it, and I still carried on keeping Scott downstairs to fall asleep. I could never tell any of my friends that I did that because they wouldn't understand. They were all 'normal', they didn't have to worry every night that their child went to bed that this is it, this is the night they are going to be sick. I had to go through that every night, to me every night as soon as it was dark Scott was going to be sick! I just wanted to be a normal mum, I wanted to be able to put Scott to bed and not worry, but I couldn't do that. So it carried on, Scott would fall asleep on the sofa, he didn't know any different (bless him) and we got on with our lives.

New Year's Eve 2004, we went to a party. We had to take our own drink, so I took my wine. I knew what my limit was and that was what I drank. I was okay, felt a bit merry, but okay. We went home, we put Scott to bed, and we went to bed and then the bed started to spin. *Oh no.* How can this be happening? I only drank what I know is okay for me to drink. Then I felt this whoosh come over me. I said to Kev, I am going to be sick. He came with me to the bathroom telling me it is okay, let it out and then I will feel better. As usual I tried to fight it, as you do! But then I was so sick, like never before, and I can remember Kev laughing, not at me being sick but the toilet seat kept falling on my head (like I said earlier, funny how you remember these funny little thoughts). I was crying like a baby, didn't want it to happen, but it did, and after one final go I felt better and went to bed and slept. The next morning I sort of remembered what had happened, but I was still confused as to how I had been ill. I took Taz to the beach and phoned my mate who had the party and told her about it, and was chatting and feeling okay, had a chat and went home. Got home and I said to Kev that I didn't feel well again and that I thought I was going to be sick again…oh my God, was I sick! But this was worse, it was in the morning. Last night I couldn't really remember what was happening, but it was right in my face this morning, I knew exactly what was happening and I was scared, really really scared! After a few times of throwing up I went back to bed. Kev told Scott that I had a bad headache. I had to keep calling to Kev because I thought I was going to do it again, but I didn't…phew…but felt really ill all day. I am sure that someone must have put something in my drink because I knew my limit, I knew how much I could drink, and that's what I had done, but I was so ill! But with me being so sick some people said to me, there, you have done it now, you know you can cope, and they thought I would be okay then, but it didn't make any difference to me. If anything it made me a whole lot worse. I fear being sick even more because it has happened recently. I know what it is like, I can remember and I hate everything about it. Some people seem to cope once they have done the dreaded deed, but not me! I am such a baby that I had to have Kev with me, I was so frightened. Scared isn't the word.

Things carried on the same. Scott would go to bed, and I would also have to go so that I was close by, or he would have to sleep on the sofa so I could stay downstairs. Kev was really understanding about this, although he did often say it wasn't good for Scott to fall asleep on the sofa all the time because he was getting into the habit of not wanting to go to bed, even if I was up there with him. Again, I felt such a bad mum; all I wanted was to be a 'normal' mum. I used to hear my friends say that it was so nice when the kids were in bed and they could sit down and relax for the evening. That didn't happen for me, when Scott was in bed was when I used to not relax, and it is still the same today.

Scott is nine years old now, it is 22 October 2006 and I still worry when he goes to bed. No one knows this (apart from Kev and my mum). I find it so hard to sit downstairs when Scott goes to bed. If he is in bed early and is watching a DVD then that is fine, but as soon as that goes off I have to go to bed too. I have to be upstairs, and it must have become a habit for Scott because he now doesn't like to be upstairs when I am downstairs, because he doesn't know any different, that is all he knows. He has never been to a mate's for a sleepover, not because I won't let him, but because he doesn't want to, and *yes* I do feel a very bad mum!

I have managed to stay downstairs a couple of evenings. Scott has been so tired he hasn't realised I am still downstairs, but when that has happened I have said to Kev, look, I am still here, I am downstairs, I know it is so stupid, something that people do every day, but to me it was a *big* step. I am still trying to keep it up and stay down, even if it is just for half an hour. Little steps will lead to bigger steps, I hope.

All I have to do then is to try and not live in fear that I am going to catch a bug when it is going around. I am getting better. My main concern at the moment is coping and dealing with my son, Scott. He is my world and I am happy to say that I have been with him while he is being sick. I don't like it, but I have done it, and that is all that matters to me, being there for my son.

Organisations and Online Resources

Note: By listing these organisations and online resources, neither I nor my publisher are implying any endorsement of the services or resources offered by them. There are several online resources out there that offer 'cures' for emetophobia, but I urge sufferers to be very careful when parting with money and always consult your doctor before embarking on treatment.

UK

Basement Project
PO Box 5
Abergavenny
Wales WP7 5XW
www.basementproject.co.uk
Publications, groups and workshops for people who self-harm.

British Association for Counsellors and Psychotherapy (BACP)
BACP House
15 St John's Business Park
Lutterworth LE17 4HB
Tel: 0870 443 5252
www.bacp.co.uk
Details of practitioners in your area and useful information.

EmetOnline.co.uk
www.emetonline.co.uk

This website aims to support not just emetophobic sufferers but also their family members. It has useful pages of information detailing films to be avoided with 'sick scenes' in and has the usual FAQ, personal stories and latest news. Free.

Emetophobia Online
www.emetonline.co.uk

A personal site ran by an emetophobic sufferer. This site is more information based, but has a great page of notes about her counselling sessions and what challenges she set herself. There is a questionnaire, also medical notes and a page from her partner. Free.

Gut Reaction
www.gut-reaction.freeserve.co.uk

This site was set up by Linda Dean. It is UK based but has members from around the globe. It covers all the latest news and research regarding emetophobia and you can order an information CD from them. Also has an extremely friendly and useful forum for members. Free.

Institute for Neuro-Physiological Psychology
www.inpp.org.uk

Based in Chester, this site covers many disorders such as dyspraxia and Asperger's syndrome, but also covers anxiety and phobias in adults. Aimed at adults, parents or teachers.

Mind
www.mind.org.uk
A charity involved with mental health.

National Phobics Society

Zion Community Resource Centre
339 Stretford Road
Hulme
Manchester
M15 4ZY
Tel: 08444 775 774
Fax: 0161 226 7727
www.phobics-society.org.uk

NPS is a national registered charity formed 30 years ago by a sufferer of agoraphobia for those affected by anxiety disorders. Today it is still a user-led organisation, run by sufferers and ex-sufferers of anxiety disorders supported by a high-profile medical advisory panel.

National Self-Harm Network
PO Box 7264
Nottingham NG1 6WJ
www.nshn.co.uk

Survivor-led organisation supporting those who self-harm.

The Samaritans
The Upper Mill
Kingston Road
Ewell
Surrey KT17 2AF
Tel: 09457 90 90 90 (24-hour advice line)
www.samaritans.org.uk

Confidential emotional support. The website allows you to find your local branch and also gives all their contact information and details of their 24-hour advice line.

USA

Emotional Freedom Techniques
www.emofree.com

Site deals with the practice of Emotional Freedom Techniques (EFT). It describes what EFT is and how it can help you, listing practitioners in your area.

International Emetophobia Society
www.emetophobia.org

This is a forum-based site that has members from around the world. Very friendly. There are discussion arenas, chatrooms and FAQ pages. Free.

International

Anxiety Treatment Australia
www.anxietyaustralia.com.au

Site provides information about anxiety disorders, treatment options and psychologists who treat anxiety disorders, support groups and resources.

Mental Health Channel
www.mentalhealthchannel.net/phobias

A catch-all site that goes into great detail about different aspects of mental health but has one particular section on phobias. Also deals with panic attacks.

Social Phobia/Social Anxiety Association
www.socialphobia.org

Site deals with social phobia, with pages of information and help.